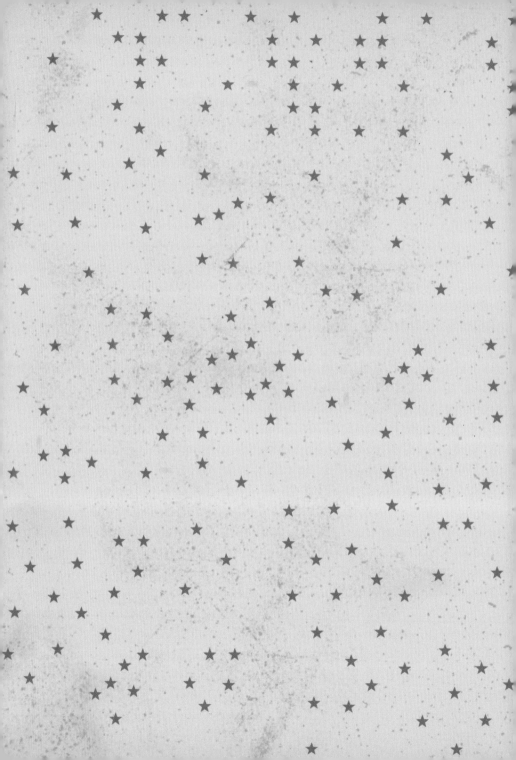

This journal belongs to

The LORD called Samuel; and he said, "Here I am."

★ ★ ★ ★ ★

1 SAMUEL 3:4 NASB

Introduction

God quietly called for Samuel when he was a boy in the still of the night. He came to Elijah on the mountaintop in a gentle wind. Jesus gave Himself to the crowds but also called His disciples to Him in solitude.

God calls us to Him, desires us to come to Him with open hands and feet ready to go where He leads. As we faithfully step out, in our imperfect path of trying, failing, and trying again, He remains faithful. As we pursue Him in all our weakness, He will reveal more and more of His plan and bring us to the abundant life, joy, and purpose He has waiting for us.

We love because He first loved us. We go and do and follow because He asks us to. There are so many areas of life that can be handed over to Him. Let your journey lead you to be ready for His call. "Here I am, Lord. I'm ready."

Yes, I Am Able

★ ★ ★ ★ ★

READ ISAIAH 29:16.

In Auschwitz, the Nazi death camp, ten men were sentenced to death by starvation as punishment for the escape of another prisoner. One of the men cried out, asking that he be permitted to live for his family's sake. Upon hearing his plea, a priest named Maximilian Kolbe volunteered to take the man's place. He died two weeks later as a result of his sacrifice.

Most of us cannot imagine being brave enough to make such a sacrifice. Kolbe, however, had been following God since childhood and had allowed the Lord to mold his spirit for many years. He was able to say, "Lord, I am able"—able to serve, able to love, able to give even his life.

If we allow God to shape our spirits, we too will be prepared to say, "Lord, we are able," in reply to whatever He asks of us.

Mold my spirit, Lord, so that I will always serve You.

Follow Me

★ ★ ★ ★ ★

READ JOHN 12:23-26.

Follow Me." Two simple words uttered by a passing Jewish teacher called the fishermen, two brothers, a tax collector. All who heard Jesus's command followed without question. Did the disciples know who He was? Did they know where they were going? Surely they couldn't have predicted that they would follow Him to heal the sick. They couldn't have known they would follow Him as He fed the multitudes with a boy's lunch. They couldn't have guessed that He would teach them a new covenant, wash their feet, and take their place on a cross. Yet they followed anyway.

They healed people in His name. They recorded His teachings, spread the gospel of love, and remained faithful even unto death.

All this the disciples learned by serving God, loving their neighbor, and remaining faithful to Jesus's two-word invitation: follow Me.

God, help me to follow You today and every day.

Come as You Are

★ ★ ★ ★ ★

READ EPHESIANS 1:4–7.

Are you procrastinating in accepting Christ or confessing sin because you feel you haven't "cleaned up" enough yet? Walking in a manner worthy of the gospel requires dependence on Jesus; it has little to do with what we feel we're capable of on our own. We can never clean up enough to be good enough for salvation.

In Judges 6, the Lord reassured a doubtful Gideon to go on in the strength he had and let God do the rest. That's His promise to us too—to provide whatever is required, if we'll just step out in faith to live in a way that will bring Him glory.

The Holy Spirit will guide, convict, protect, and grow us as we submit to a relationship with Him. God's grace and mercy will triumph over our shortcomings.

Abba, You could have given up on me but You didn't;
You waited. Thank You.

Patience

READ ROMANS 15:1–5.

As Christians, when we think about the consequences of our sin, we are quickly—with thankful hearts—reminded of the saving work of Christ in our lives and how we don't have to pay the penalty. Through His sacrifice, Christ demonstrated an inconceivable love for us.

Christ is incredibly patient. Some of us run away from Him, regularly stumbling into sin, and others struggle with faith. Nevertheless, Christ patiently waits for us, helping us overcome hurdles and drawing us closer to Himself.

Through Christ's patient example, we are inspired to also demonstrate patience. How can we who have received such loving patience not look kindly and graciously toward those who have offended us?

Our Christ-infused hearts will stir within us an abiding love for others.

Father, help me to demonstrate the same patience
toward others that You have demonstrated toward me.

Thank You, Jesus

★ ★ ★ ★ ★

READ JOHN 18:4-9.

We need only read slowly and carefully the familiar accounts of Christ's crucifixion in the four Gospels to be overwhelmed by His sacrifice for us. He was innocent of all crimes, yet false charges were leveled against Him. A lead-tipped whip tore apart His back. A crown of long, sharp thorns was crushed into His scalp. A heavy cross was placed on His shredded back to carry to His own crucifixion. Nails dug into His wrists and feet.

Didn't the Jews know that this was their promised Messiah? Didn't the soldiers recognize that this was no ordinary man? Obviously not. But Jesus, knowing who He was and why He came, willingly submitted to all of the torture. He suffered and died and conquered death so that we too could have the final victory.

Lord Jesus, may I never forget what You did for me at Calvary.

A Blind Leap?

★ ★ ★ ★ ★

READ ROMANS 5:1–2.

While it's true that faith involves making an intellectual assent to the truth of God revealed in creation and history, we can have an intellectual belief in Jesus but not have saving faith—a faith that promises eternal rescue from sin.

Saving faith comes down to Jesus. What do we believe about Jesus's death on the cross and resurrection from the dead? Do we say with our minds and our hearts, "Yes, I believe in Christ and receive what He has done for me"?

At some point, we all have to answer that question. For some, saying yes may feel like taking a leap, a wild jump, in the dark. But it isn't.

We can trust our souls to God because of what Jesus has done for us.

We can say, "Yes! I believe," without fear.

Thank You, heavenly Father, for revealing Yourself to me.
I believe in You.

Seeing God in the Darkness

★ ★ ★ ★ ★

READ PSALM 30:5.

The dark night of the soul is a time when God seems distant, when our souls seem lost. But purpose exists in the darkness. In any worthwhile venture, pain precedes gain, hurt precedes health, cleansing precedes completeness. During these dark seasons, God works in our inner being so we will turn from destructive habits to develop Christlike character. Like polluted water that flows through a filter, our souls will be purified.

Often when the night is blackest, we feel God has abandoned us. Yet God is working even then. Like the moon hidden by an eclipse, God is present even when He's not visible.

During the dark times, God is at work. We will see Him again. And, better, we will be cleansed, made right, made whole. Hang on.

Endure the night. Joy comes in the morning.

Do Your cleansing work in my heart, O God. I will trust You.

The Face of Jesus Christ

★ ★ ★ ★

READ 2 CORINTHIANS 4:6.

How amazing it is that God wants you to know His heart. He wants you to know how much He loves you. The Creator of the world, the Holy One who is above and beyond anything you can imagine, wants to know you.

How do you know the love of God? How do you know the Father's heart? The answer is found in the face of Jesus Christ.

In 2 Corinthians 4, Paul gives a clue to that truth. God has given light in the darkness, and that light shines in our hearts so we can know the glory of God through the face of Jesus. It is Jesus who gives the perfect picture of God. When you know Jesus, you know God. He wants you to know His heart.

He wants you to know how much He loves you. And when you know Him, you can't help but return that love to Him.

Thank You, Father, for showing Your face to me in Jesus.
I desire to love You with all my heart.

....

....

....

....

....

....

....

....

....

The Living Word

★ ★ ★ ★

READ COLOSSIANS 3:12–17.

Nurses and doctors report that when aged saints are on their deathbeds and under heavy sedation, they often will revert to their childhood. They recite memory verses learned during vacation Bible school, or they sing "Jesus Loves Me" or "This Little Light of Mine."

Colossians 3:16 says, "Let the word of Christ dwell in you richly" (NKJV). Such blessings can happen when we have made the Word of God a living, active, vibrant part of our lives, judging every action, every deed, every thought by what the Lord has instilled in our hearts. David said, "Your word I have hidden in my heart" (Psalm 119:11 NKJV). Christ living in us gives us a contentment that unbelievers cannot understand. But it is real. It is comforting. It is genuine.

Lord, I rejoice in knowing that Your Spirit permeates my very being.

True Belief

★ ★ ★ ★ ★

READ JAMES 2:22.

Nietzsche said God is dead. While Nietzsche, an atheist, wasn't interested in embracing Christian beliefs, his words are a good reminder of what can happen when a society sets God aside. People execute their faith and turn their back on the Savior. They stop pursuing God with resolve and passion. Even those who go to church and claim a religion can quickly veer off course if they stop at belief but do not let it affect their lives.

Belief is more than just a position or a realization. We were designed for a relationship with Christ and we find our ultimate purpose and meaning in Him. True belief is about the journey through life in relationship with God. True belief is alive and active, affecting our lives today and every day.

Let my belief in You resonate in my life today, Lord

....

....

....

....

....

....

....

....

....

....

True Transcendence

★ ★ ★ ★ ★

READ ISAIAH 1:18.

How do we transcend ourselves? Great thinkers have been trying to answer that question for centuries, often telling us to look within and rely on the resources deep inside ourselves. Indeed, we are endowed with inner qualities that go beyond genetics and physiology. We have something intangible about us, something spiritual and eternal that surpasses biological and chemical matter. But it's far from pure or strong; it's sinful and in need of cleansing. Only God, the Creator, can recreate us. He made us and knows our true nature. We are nothing without Him. With Him, we are capable of leaving our human failings behind.

Our true transformation is initiated and completed by God alone. We transcend ourselves not by looking within but by looking at the cross and the only Savior who can make us all He created us to be.

Jesus, help me to see my deep and abiding need for You.

Hand in Hand

★ ★ ★ ★ ★

READ ISAIAH 41:13.

As the mother and her young child prepare to cross a busy street, the mother grasps her child's hand. A young man bends his knee before the love of his life and puts a ring on her finger. An elderly couple walks hand in hand as the two stroll down a sandy beach. With our hands we touch, we hold, we love, we protect.

Remember the first time you reached out to God and put your hand in His? Your Father's hand is always there, reaching out to you, holding you, loving you, protecting you. He has not released His grasp. When your prayer of faith touched the heart of God, Jesus took your hand in His with a promise to hold it forever.

Lord, thank You for the promise of Your hand
throughout my life.

Countermeasures

READ 1 JOHN 4:4.

Suffering is a universal language. We can't escape pain. Plans go wrong. Troubles come. Our bodies wear out. We live in a fallen world, and sometimes the pressure paralyzes us. Deep ocean waters can crush a submarine made of thick steel, but little fish with the thinnest layer of skin swim there without a care in the world. Why aren't they crushed? They have an internal pressure that perfectly corresponds to the pressure on the outside. God gives them what they need to swim in the deep places.

When faced with the pressure of suffering, we don't need skin made of steel; we need a power inside us that corresponds to the pressure around us. That power comes from the presence of Jesus, who lives within us. Surrounded by pressure? Sense the presence of Jesus. Then rest secure in Him.

*Lord, I trust Your countermeasures within to overcome
the mounting pressures without.*

Byways and Back Lanes

★ ★ ★ ★

READ JEREMIAH 6:16.

Where are the byways and back lanes of your heart? What grows along those paths? Too often they are somberly lit, allowing the darkness to hide the actions and thoughts that would embarrass us if seen in the light.

Too often we slip there. A temptation. An angry outburst. A feeling of hopelessness or helplessness. A desire unfulfilled. We justify our actions and walk down the shadowy path. Only too late do we realize that we have slipped away from the presence of God.

In His presence is light. In His presence the pathway is clear and the way is lit by God's Word. As the psalmist wrote, "Your word is a lamp to my feet and a light to my path" (Psalm119:105 NKJV).

Let's close off the byways and back lanes and stay on the path. God has promised that He will show us the way; we merely need to walk in it.

Lord, let me stay on the clear path, the one marked out for me.

The Greatest Gift

★ ★ ★ ★ ★

READ ROMANS 8:37-39.

We take another promotion, seeking status in our work. We build bigger nest eggs, seeking power in our money. We take exotic vacations, seeking adventure in our trips. We relive our past through our children, seeking a lost youth.

We are looking for ourselves as though we were searching for hidden treasure. Yet our gift is the presence of Jesus. Consider His love for us. Despite our faults, He runs to us. Seeing our sin, He forgives us. Knowing we deserve death, He grants us life. Our identity is hidden in the love and mercy of God. In Him, our veneers of self-preservation are sanded off; the scaffolding of stuff holding us up is removed. We are loved by God. What better gift could we find?

Thank You, Lord, for Your gift of love.
In it I find myself.

Love Divinely

★ ★ ★ ★ ★

READ ROMANS 8:35-39.

Throughout the ages humanity has been drawn to the image of the eagle. Nobility in particular often used this bird to represent their strength.

God has been portrayed in literature as the Divine Eagle who soars above all, including kings and emperors. And yet surprisingly, this Divine Eagle, so mighty and majestic, longs to draw us to Himself. In fact, His love for us is so great that He suffered and died in order to give us an eternal home. How shall we respond to so great a love? By offering our lifelong love in return.

Be encouraged to open your heart to God, to dwell each day under the wings of the One who gave His life for you and longs to teach you to soar with Him.

Thank You, Father, for loving me so fully.

....

....

....

....

....

....

....

....

....

....

In the Waiting

★ ★ ★ ★ ★

READ ISAIAH 30:18.

Patience is a gift. Many say it's one they don't have. Regardless, we are forced to wait. In the store checkout line, as the boss makes a final decision, at the doctor's office, at the busy intersection. Sometimes we must wait in order to wait some more.

Waiting in the daily details is an unpleasant part of life. And when a mundane job remains mundane, or physical pain clings like a bad shirt, or an anticipated situation refuses to evolve as we dreamed it would, questions arise. What is God doing? Why doesn't He fix it? What's His purpose in allowing the unwanted circumstances to persist?

Your daily routine that seems to never change may last for just one more day. But it could be yours for another month, another year, or even longer. What will you do in the waiting? Dear friend, take a new look at this season. Fight your frustrations and trust that this place of preparation is of great importance

Lord, change my perspective so that I can see significance as I wait.

He Carries It All

★ ★ ★ ★ ★

READ MATTHEW 11:28-30.

The famous poem "Footprints" reminds us that in life's most difficult seasons, Jesus does not abandon us; rather, He picks us up and carries us.

We are amazed by the picture of a burden-bearing Savior. He took our sin upon Himself so that we might have freedom. He takes up our shame so that we are no longer hindered by it. What other burdens has He taken upon Himself rather than letting them fall to us? Whatever is loading you down today, you need carry it no longer. Jesus will scoop up the weight in one arm and put His other arm around your tired shoulders. Gently He'll remind you that it is for these very things that He sacrificed His life. Today, feel Him removing the weight of your burden and holding you near.

Thank You, Savior, for carrying my burdens.

The Way Home

★ ★ ★ ★

READ JOHN 1:1, 14.

Have you ever become separated from your group in an unfamiliar place? Your heart pumps faster. Your palms grow clammy. Your thoughts run wild.

Lostness is not just a physical reality; it is a spiritual fact too. When we are lost, we need someone to show us the way home. Verbal communication is not good enough; personal help is what we long for—someone to take us by the hand to guide us home.

That's the message of Christianity. God dropped everything to seek out and rescue lost humans. It boggles the mind that God would send His own Son so that a lost humanity would find its way to Him. Yet that's exactly what God did. Try to find a parallel story in another religion. Can't do it, can you? Christianity is God finding us and bringing us home.

Thank You, Lord, for saving me.

First in Your Heart

★ ★ ★ ★ ★

READ NAHUM 1:2-6.

When a bride and groom stand before the altar, they promise love and devotion "till death do us part." How can they make such a promise? How can they know that they will always feel this way?

It's easy in the beauty of the wedding ceremony; unfortunately, it's not easy when the pressures of life mount in the coming years. But that's just the thing—the promise is not to feel that way forever, the promise is to live that way forever. To always act with love and devotion, regardless of how we feel at the moment.

Every one of us longs to be loved—to be first in someone else's thoughts, to sense devotion that overwhelms us with joy. God wants us to put Him first in exactly the same way. To live with love and devotion, regardless of the doubts, the problems, the fears. He wants to be first in our lives.

Lord, help me to remember that You merit my total love and loyalty.

Come Away

★ ★ ★ ★ ★

READ SONG OF SONGS 2:10.

Put down the phone. Push away the keyboard. Turn off the television. God invites you to stop and spend time with Him alone. Like an excited fiancé who wants nothing but to enjoy time with his beloved, God seeks you out to simply be with Him. He doesn't need pious prayers. He doesn't ask for lofty commitments or ritualistic practices. He asks for you. You, there in the middle of work's madness. You, tired and longing for someone to notice you. You, broken and distant. He wants your company and will not tire in searching you out.

Sometimes God's silence compels us to run and find Him. Other times, the glowing sun outside the kitchen window signals us to drop the ordinary and be captivated by Him...just for a moment. Bring your open heart today and allow yourself to be drawn near to Him.

Extraordinary God, I long to spend time with You today.

No Posers

★ ★ ★ ★

READ GALATIANS 5:16.

The Urban Dictionary defines poser as someone who "tries to fit in but with exaggeration." You've probably encountered such individuals. They desperately want to blend into the group, but it rarely happens because they are so self-conscious.

Posers mingle in the Christian world. In public, they tell us life is great and their smiles come freely—for a few short hours. Eventually, though, they must retreat and reenergize, because relying on self-righteousness runs even the best intentions into the ground.

Are we guilty of posing, of putting on a good face? We don't have to keep trying so hard. Let's become consumed with Christ and who He wants to be in our lives, going forward in the confidence that He is with us. His Spirit enables us to find our place.

Lord Jesus, empower me to relax today in Your love and acceptance.

Beauty from Weakness

★ ★ ★ ★

READ PHILIPPIANS 4:10-13.

We humans are prone to weakness. Our mortal bodies are susceptible to disease and injury, while our emotions and priorities can easily get out of control.

Hymn writer Fanny Crosby was familiar with frailty. Blind from infancy in an era when blindness could mean an institutionalized existence, no one imagined God had plans for her to become a famous songstress.

Part of the Christian life is the calling God places upon us, and often that calling seems impossible. But God uses our weaknesses to draw us to Him. For when He requires something of us beyond our ability, we are forced to depend on Him and only Him. Our emotions and priorities cannot be relied on, nor can our physical bodies.

When we completely surrender, He will use our weaknesses, our blindness—all our frailties—to make us something beautiful for the kingdom of God.

Use my weaknesses to further Your kingdom, Father.

Praying for the Salvation of Family Members

★ ★ ★ ★

READ JOHN 3:16-17.

Very few of us come from families where every family member knows Jesus. If you do, you are extremely blessed. The rest of us come from families in which lives transformed through salvation in Jesus are present only sporadically. Regardless of how many of our family members know Jesus, we earnestly pray for the rest to come to faith.

When we accepted the gift of salvation through Jesus Christ, the love of Christ filled our hearts, causing us to desire what He desires. Paramount among the desires of Christ now implanted in us is the desire to see lost people find their eternal home in Christ. What better place to start than with the Christ-infused compulsion to pray for and witness to those closest to us—our own family members?

Father, give me a Christ-infused desire to pray for the salvation of my family.

Love in Action

★ ★ ★ ★ ★

READ LUKE 6:35-36.

Mercy is far more than nice thoughts, a kind disposition, sympathetic feelings, or a loving demeanor. Mercy realizes that someone is hurting and gets involved.

Just as Jesus took on human flesh and lived among us, experiencing our pain and limitations, mercy gets inside people's skin. The merciful see a need, are moved by that need, and meet that need. Mercy helps the hurting, cares for the sick, brings a cup of cold water to the thirsty, reaches out to the untouchable, forgives the fallen, and is patient with the peculiar.

We are to be merciful because God has shown mercy to us. He has met our needs, eased our ache, and saved our souls—all while sharing our humanness through Jesus. We respond by showing mercy to others. And in that act, we receive even more mercy from God.

Lord, help me to follow Your example and be merciful.

Ideally Created

★ ★ ★ ★ ★

READ MATTHEW 5:16.

Have you ever felt that you could be more effective for God if only you were more of an extrovert...or you had additional financial resources...or you had the gift of evangelism?

Here's something to consider: we would do well to spend less time trying to be like other people and more time discovering God's plan for us as individuals.

Who are the people God has placed in your life to whom you can show His light? What talents has God given you, and how might He use them to draw others to Himself? What resources has God provided that you could invest in His kingdom?

God made you to fit His plan and purpose for you. He has given you a unique circle of influence and a unique approach to being His appointed light in this dark world. Ask Him to show you how.

Thank You, Father, that You created me just as I am.

....

....

....

....

....

....

....

....

....

Answering God's Call

★ ★ ★ ★ ★

READ HEBREWS 12:1-2.

How often, within the first few minutes of meeting someone, have you been asked, "What kind of work do you do?" It's not surprising, really, since in our culture, a person's work is closely tied to their identity.

However, the definition of vocation is "a calling"—something well beyond just a job. While God clearly designed us with abilities and interests that help us flourish in certain lines of work, we must not lose sight of the fact that answering His call is far more than finding the right career. Answering God's call means saying yes to His offer of salvation and then investing all that we are, all that we do, and all that we have in living each day for Him.

That calling gives purpose and meaning to life. That calling answers all the whys of our existence—and even gives us a reason for getting up and going to work each day.

How will you answer God's call today?

Dear Father, help me to say yes to Your call each day.

Who We Are

★ ★ ★ ★ ★

READ JOHN 15:5.

Who are we apart from God? We are everything, or we are nothing. Everything (or so we think)—if we tell ourselves we don't need His help and rely on our own strength. Nothing—if we realize our utter dependence on Him and our place in the created order.

Are we willing to admit that we are nothing so that Jesus can be everything to us? Or are we holding on to areas of our lives we think we can handle without Him? Believing in God doesn't always mean we trust Him fully. But He is there for us, if we will accept His grace and appreciate how lost we are without Him.

Let your life go, into the loving arms of the Savior.

Lord Jesus, may I become nothing
so You can be everything in my life.

Pop Quiz

★ ★ ★ ★ ★

READ GALATIANS 5:19–23.

A car cuts you off and you miss your exit, making you late for your job interview. You finally arrive and rush up the elevator, only to realize you left your résumé at home. Someone in your small group gossiped, telling your embarrassing struggle to close friends. Your in-laws gave you money for your birthday. You buy something special with it, only to find that your check for the water bill has bounced, and the bank fees leave you with nothing for groceries.

Time to sing the blues, or time to trust the Lord? We can trust Him through it all. God may be using these tests to find out whether we love Him more than our friends, our job opportunity, or our bottom line.

It is in this moment—during the test—that we find out what's in our hearts.

Have my heart, Lord, I want to trust You more.

Anything, Anyone, Anytime

★ ★ ★ ★ ★

READ EXODUS 3:1-12.

You may be a lover, not a fighter. But chances are you've still resorted to "boxing"—that familiar tendency to put others in a box: I can't visit that church member in the hospital; that's the pastor's responsibility. Why pick up my mess in the church? The janitor gets paid to do it. I'm not going to serve on the worship team; that's the music minister's job.

We miss so much when we put limitations on ourselves or others. But we especially miss out when we try to limit God Himself. God can work through anything or anyone at any time. Remember Balaam's donkey? It spoke words of warning. Remember Moses? God called him from a burning bush. Remember Daniel? God shut the lions' mouths. Remember the earthquake that freed Paul from prison? God did that too.

Fortunately, God will not be put in a box. You can trust Him to do the impossible. He may just break you out of your own box as He is breaking free of His.

Break me out of my box, God. Do the impossible.

....

....

....

....

....

....

....

....

Resetting the Treadmill

★ ★ ★ ★ ★

READ MARK 1:35.

Work, school, family, community. There are some days when an underlying rhythm seems to keep it all running smoothly. Other days, though, all those commitments seem to be speeding up with each mile we run.

Speed has become the taskmaster in this digital age. We move so fast and handle so many tasks on any given day that we hardly even notice any of our accomplishments. Worse, our connection with God starts to slip. The light of His work in our lives rushes by in an unrecognizable flash.

Still, Jesus is calling. He beckons us to a speed of His design and perfection. He invites us to reset our pace to keep Him in our line of vision, just as He did with His Father. As Jesus talked and prayed with God, He was refreshed for ministry and prepared for His Father's pace.

Take some time to refuel, refresh, and regroup today. Hit the RESET button on your treadmill. Jesus is waiting to help you move in step with Him.

Lord, help me to experience fullness in You today.

A Divine Hunger

★ ★ ★ ★ ★

READ PHILIPPIANS 3:8.

It is almost impossible to fathom how a world so full of information can be lacking in understanding. And yet it is. We are challenged to pursue advanced degrees, prompted to keep up with the newest trends, urged to stay competent in the latest technology. But have such endeavors filled our lives with meaning and hope? No. One problem is that these endeavors—as worthy as they are—aren't big enough to capture our hearts.

A believer has a more compelling goal: to know God. Not just to know about God or gather facts concerning God or memorize a creed regarding God, but to have a relationship with the living God. The difference is as vast as knowing the recipe for your favorite pie—and actually sinking your teeth into a fresh-out-of-the-oven slice. Formulas cannot do justice to the experience.

Once we know God, once we experience Him, we will only hunger for more of Him. Let's pursue Him with all our passion.

Dear God, I want to know You more and more.

Streams of Thought

★ ★ ★ ★

READ 2 CORINTHIANS 10:4-6.

As soon as the words were out of your mouth, you wished you could take them back. You hadn't meant to think those things, let alone say them. But now you've done both!

Some days our thoughts are beautiful and clear, like a mountain stream flowing gently between green valleys. All is well with our world and everyone in it. Other days our thoughts are like raging rapids—full of churning turmoil and unexpected dangers. Interactions with people leave us angry, tense. Circumstances force us to navigate the waters of loneliness or sorrow. Situations tempt us to be reckless and reflect on things that are impure or unlovely.

On those rough-water days, how essential it is to take all our thoughts captive. Peace is ours when we submit our thoughts to Christ and resist the enemy. Today, let God calm your thoughts with His truth, His light, His love. He's ready to quiet your mind and your heart.

Keep my thoughts in the streams of truth, light, and love today, God.

Armed and Ready

★ ★ ★ ★ ★

READ EPHESIANS 6:10.

Where do we go to find the ammunition needed for today's battle? With evil spiritual forces rallied against us and an unkind world counteracting us in every way, we could perhaps excuse ourselves for going AWOL (or at least for staying far from the front lines). We feel we do not have the weapons we need; we feel outgunned and outnumbered.

But we are never outdone when we have properly prepared for battle through a life of quiet, personal worship. Only in the hidden times with God, when we stand before Him in worship, lost in wonder, captivated by His majesty and holiness—only then are we prepared for the battle.

In the quiet, Lord, I worship You.
Arm me for today's battle.

Divine Nature

★ ★ ★ ★

READ JOHN 16:7.

Don't copy the behavior and customs of this world, but let God transform you into a new person" (Romans 12:2 NLT). Try as we might, that change—that transformation—is out of our reach. We vow to defeat the impulse to judge, the flare of anger, the habit that threatens our health. We stand at the door of need... need for a helper. A helper who took on earthly wrappings but whose divine nature did not die. Jesus's divine nature joined with our humanity to empower us to be transformed into new creations.

Be encouraged if transformation is out of your reach. Invite the Holy Spirit to lead you, to be your Helper. Let Jesus's divine nature live in you.

Indwell me, Lord, with Your Holy Spirit.
Fill me anew each day.

It Doesn't Make Sense

★ ★ ★ ★ ★

READ COLOSSIANS 2:1–15.

Christianity is full of paradoxes: one must die to live, give to have, mourn to be happy, be poor to be rich, surrender to be victorious. But no greater paradox exists than Jesus's cross: love birthed in hate, beauty arising from ugliness, a good man dying so bad men could be saved.

The cross was the Roman Empire's torturous instrument of death. Victims hung suspended between heaven and earth. The crossbeams stood in paradox—the vertical beam jutted upward toward heaven, like a champion thrusting his fist into the air, satisfying the demands of God's holiness; the horizontal beam reached outward toward the earth like a father's arms, signifying the embrace of God's love.

It doesn't make sense, does it? But that doesn't make it any less true. Let us delight in the cross.

Thank You, Jesus, for the cross.

....

....

....

....

....

....

....

....

The Cross

★ ★ ★ ★ ★

READ LUKE 22:39–44.

Sharing doesn't come easily. We learn to say, "It's mine," early and then say it all too often. Even the most well-meaning Christians can find their hearts hardened when someone asks for something.

What if Christ had been like that, saying no to His Father's plan for the ages? There would have been no cross—and no salvation. But Jesus was always thinking of others, from making sure guests at the wedding in Cana had enough to drink to ensuring that Peter didn't sink into the Sea of Galilee.

The ultimate example of Christ's selflessness was Calvary, of course. The cross stands as the offer of salvation to all humanity. No one person owns it. It belongs to all.

God, I am so grateful for Your willingness to share
what cost You so much: Your Son.

Unlimited Access

★ ★ ★ ★ ★

READ HEBREWS 10:19-22.

In the Old Testament, the curtain in the temple prevented God's people from seeing into the Most Holy Place where His presence dwelt. But the New Testament records that when Jesus died on the cross, the curtain ripped in two, signifying our unlimited access to God through Christ.

We may easily assent to this amazing truth, but do we act on it? Do we enter God's presence throughout our day? Do you see Him, know Him, live with Him ever in our midst? Or do we hang our own curtains that prevent us from enjoying Him?

Perhaps we have allowed our self-focus to become a barrier that keeps us from God. It's possible to even become too self-sufficient to want to be with God—or too full of self-pity.

God wants us to see Him and live with Him and draw life from His smile. Look up. Because that curtain was torn by Jesus, you can see God smiling.

Forgive me, Lord, for the things that I let keep me from You.

Do You See What God Sees?

★ ★ ★ ★ ★

READ ISAIAH 61:10.

Look in the mirror. What do you see? Are your sins written all over your face? Pride? Envy? Lack of forgiveness? Prejudice? Judging? Anger? Bitterness?

Look again and see what God sees. Beauty. Loveliness. Perfection. How can this be? Because when God looks at you, He sees His Son. He sees the shed blood of His beloved one given for you. He sees you clothed in righteousness.

A sixteenth-century hymn says it well: "Jesus, Thy blood and righteousness, Thy beauty are my glorious dress." What God sees is beauty that is not our own. It was bought with a price. The precious blood of Jesus was shed for believers to be right with God...to be clothed with Christ.

Be beautiful. Wear Christ.

Jesus, let the mirror of my life reflect You.

Loosen Your Grip

★ ★ ★ ★ ★

READ MATTHEW 13:10–17.

Do you cling to the God you've always known? Maybe He's the God your parents and Sunday school teachers taught you about when you were young. He might be the very same God you trusted for salvation at a tender age. You are comfortable with this God and the ways He speaks.

Being grounded in the knowledge of such a personal God is likely the best blessing you have been given. But if your understanding of God remains the same throughout your life, your growth will be stunted.

God never changes. His attributes remain exactly the same in proportion and number for all eternity. But to a soul open to deeper understanding, God reveals more of Himself. Where is He working that broadens your understanding of Him? Look, see, and understand that He is much more than you can comprehend. You will never reach the end of knowing Him.

Loosen my grip on who I believe You are. Reveal Yourself anew.

Why Pray?

★ ★ ★ ★ ★

READ PSALM 5:1-3.

God tells us in His Word to pray about everything. Yet He already knows everything. So what is the point of prayer?

Compare it to a child who comes to a parent with a request. When we pray, we are that child—humbling ourselves before our heavenly Father, admitting our limitations, trusting His desire to provide, and acknowledging His resources.

In the process of approaching Him, in asking Him to take care of us, in making our requests known, we mature. We grow in our understanding of both ourselves and God. And we learn to trust as well.

God commands us to pray, and pray specifically, because He knows it is good for us. Our loving Father wants to help us mature in our faith through the spiritual discipline of prayer. He knows that prayer brings us closer to His heart.

*Dear Father, thank You for caring about me
as Your beloved child.*

Not My will but God's

★ ★ ★ ★ ★

READ LUKE 22:42.

Jesus didn't mince words. When facing the horror of the cross, He asked God to take it away. But then came the words that bring us to our knees: "Not my will, but yours be done." Jesus knew His prayer wasn't about getting His way; it was about doing God's will and trusting Him.

Conforming who we are to God's will is a process that takes a lifetime. The refining never ends.

Maybe you're in a situation where you're thinking, *I don't want God's will this time!* That hard conversation at home? Deductions at tax time? Choosing to give away money earmarked for a TV?

When those times come, it's time to get in God's presence and ask Him to realign your priorities—not your will, but His.

Lord, Your will is, and will always be, the best way.
Conform my will to Yours.

....

....

....

....

....

....

....

....

....

God's Masterpiece

★ ★ ★ ★

READ HEBREWS 4:12.

Masters of foreign languages require many semesters of study before they are fluent. Airplane pilots need countless hours of both simulated and actual flight before they can safely soar the skies. Authors and artists alike endure years of creating, re-creating, and being critiqued before realizing their masterpieces. Progressing in our relationship with God—learning His ways and character—takes time and practice too.

Do you want to lead a spiritually transformed life that is worthy of God's kingdom? The key is to saturate yourself in Scripture—reading it, memorizing it, studying it, meditating on it. It means taking time to pray, to worship, to be still before your Creator. As you daily immerse yourself in a relationship with the living God and a study of His Word, your life will become His masterpiece.

Give me a desire to be saturated in Scripture, Lord.

The Right Medicine

★ ★ ★ ★ ★

READ LUKE 10:30-35.

When we accidentally injure ourselves in the middle of a busy day, sometimes there's barely enough time to slap on a bandage—let alone examine it, clean it, or apply any medicine—before moving on to our next task.

Isn't it good to know that the Lord doesn't take that approach with us? As the Great Physician, He cares just as much about the cause of our pain as He does the symptoms. He won't just affix a bandage to the problem. He'll want to evaluate, assess, and examine your life. Then, with skill and precision, He will write the perfect prescription for a comprehensive treatment that will lead to your healing.

What is injured in your life today? The doctor is in, and His appointment book is open.

Lord, I give You all that ails me today.

The Darkest Night

★ ★ ★ ★ ★

READ ROMANS 8:26–27.

A young woman lay in her bed. Sleep had eluded her for hours as she tossed and turned. Her mind couldn't stop thinking about her problems at work, her shallow relationships, and, even worse, her complete lack of faith that God still cared about her. But then the moonlight shone through the blinds and illuminated her face, reminding her—as silent tears streamed down her cheeks—that the Light of the world still watched over her.

Life is sometimes like the night: with seemingly no end to the darkness, just solitude and loneliness. Problems appear larger than life, and cries to God seem to go unanswered. Paul explained in Romans 8 that at our weakest point, the Holy Spirit will speak for us, communicating what we ourselves do not know we need. After all, who knows our hearts and our needs better than the One who created us?

Thank You for Your interceding Holy Spirit, Father.

Light in a Dark Place

★ ★ ★ ★ ★

READ JOHN 8:12.

It is no secret that some days are dark. At times our darkness might be so deep that we cannot see the next step on the path—so we sit on the side of life's road, afraid to take a step because we might fall or trip or walk over the edge of a cliff.

Darkness can be frightening. But our Lord, the Light of the world, understands. In our darkest hours, He shines the brightness of His glory on our gloomy paths. When we look to the Father, He will give us light and show us the way.

When you are lonely, He is there. When you are anxious, He is there. When you see only darkness, He is there with the light of life.

Lord, no matter how things look now,
I trust that You will lighten my darkness.

Guilt-Free Happiness

★ ★ ★ ★ ★

READ PSALM 34:8–10.

It has been a long week, but today is Friday. The sun is brightly shining, with a blue sky, light wind, perfect temperature. Could it get any better?

"Could you come into my office?" your boss asks at lunchtime. "You've done great work this month. Take this afternoon off. Here are two tickets to that big show downtown. Fifth row. My treat."

On the way home, you make every green light, even that one at the complicated six-way intersection.

A good day? Believe it! Don't feel guilty. Be happy. Thank God for today (and for next Monday). And remember that He loves you—on the good days as much as on the bad days.

You are the God who loves me during tough times
and good times. Thank You!

Competing Goals and Loyalties

★ ★ ★ ★ ★

READ HEBREWS 12:1.

As men and women of faith, we thrive when we make our walk with God our top priority. But many other things compete for our attention—family, career, financial obligations, relationships. How do we manage our relationships and responsibilities without letting them distract us from God?

It is good to examine our goals and loyalties honestly and determine if we need to eliminate some of them. As you identify your priorities, ask yourself:

Am I focused on achieving something that keeps me from spending time growing in my faith?

Am I loyal to someone or something that is pulling me away from God?

Sometimes we must say no to the good in order to say yes to the best. Today, as men and women of faith, let's determine to put God first.

God, adjust my goals and loyalties so I can focus on You.

Reality Check

★ ★ ★ ★ ★

READ HEBREWS 4:14-16.

How would you describe your life right now? Does the word peace come to mind? Many believers struggle with experiencing God's peace in the midst of their real, here-and-now difficulties. We think that the only way we'll find peace is by pretending everything is just fine. But God knows the reality we each face.

Finding God's peace doesn't mean we have to deny our struggles or pretend that our lives are calm and serene. Our Lord never asks us to lie to Him, to others, or to ourselves. On the contrary, God wants us to confront our difficulties, knowing that when we approach the cross, we approach an omniscient God who is intimately aware of everything we are facing.

When God offers us His abiding peace, we can trust that He will give it to us, even in the midst of our reality.

Thank You for understanding my real life.
Help me find peace in the midst of it.

A Beggar's Kingdom

★ ★ ★ ★ ★

READ MATTHEW 18:1-5.

Everywhere you look, people are busy trying to build their own "kingdoms" of power and influence. They strive and sacrifice to make a name for themselves. Desperate to prove their independence, these men and women exhaust themselves chasing worldly success and self-sufficiency. Yet even seemingly noble intentions reflect insidious pride.

God offers us so much more than the delusion of success—He offers us His kingdom when we come helpless and humble, knowing that we cannot gain His kingdom on our own. We obtain it when we humbly accept Christ's love and sacrifice on our behalf. We come as beggars, and then we are given an esteemed place in God's kingdom as His adopted children.

We need not be too proud to accept God's charity. Only when we become beggars will we experience the riches of God's grace.

Father, let me realize how helpless I am without You.

Becoming More

★ ★ ★ ★ ★

PHILIPPIANS 3: 20-21.

The Grand Canyon is renowned for its majesty and grandeur. Two hundred seventy-seven miles long, eighteen miles wide, and up to a mile deep...few places can make a human feel so small. Yet if someone has never been to the Grand Canyon, how can we describe it? Mere words cannot capture its breathtaking beauty and magnitude.

Heaven is similarly impossible to describe adequately. Some depictions of our eternity there even make it seem boring. But God promises us something far greater: a place of eternal fulfillment. In heaven we will be more, not less, than we are here on earth. What that means, we do not yet know. But one day, we will.

We can trust that God will make our eternity better than we can even imagine.

Father, I can't wait to be with You.

Our Omnipotent God

★ ★ ★ ★ ★

READ PSALM 46.

Popular movies portray God as capricious or mock Him as weak and uncaring. As a result, people often consider God to be a distant but doting figure who doesn't pay much attention to the world or its inhabitants.

But God's Word tells a different story. We serve a God whose voice can melt the earth. His right hand upholds the UNIVERSE. He speaks, and creation rushes to obey. He knows everything. There is nothing we can hide from Him. He will not be mocked without consequence. And we cannot outwit, outrun, or outdo Him in any way.

Yet this magnificent God—this all-powerful Creator of heaven and earth—stoops to embrace us. He is the unquestionable King of everything...but He is also our Father. Knowing this, we approach His throne boldly, secure in our position as coheirs with Christ.

Help me realize just how great You are, Lord.

Our Grief, Our Joy

★ ★ ★ ★ ★

READ 1 PETER 2:21-25.

The resurrection of Christ is God's greatest act of redemptive grace. Nothing before or since has demonstrated God's love so grandly. Jesus rising from the grave signified God's triumph over death and the reconnection of humanity to the Father.

Looking back from this side of the cross, it's easy to forget the awful price our sin demanded. Because of our failure, God Himself came to save us. It's easy to forget this sobering reality: we are responsible for the murder of our Savior.

It's easy to grow desensitized to the idea that Christ had to die for us to live. How else could we hear sermons about His sacrifice without being overwhelmed with the desire to weep for the death of our Savior?

Yet, even so, our grief contrasts with joy. Though the price was high—higher than we could pay—God has saved us. Praise our Father: we are saved!

Father, thank You that Your Son's sacrifice has saved me!

Secure in Power

★ ★ ★ ★ ★

READ PHILIPPIANS 2:5–11.

There's an odd thing about power: the more powerful you are, the less you need to tell people about it. We all know by experience that the more people need to talk about themselves, the less secure they are.

Imagine for a moment, then, the immense majesty of a God so secure in His power that He is willing to be born to poor parents in a drafty barn; to mingle with dirty, flawed human beings; to be mocked, scorned, and publicly executed.

We often forget just how much dignity Jesus could have claimed. As the ruler of the universe, the King of kings would have been justified in commanding humanity to afford Him proper respect.

Yet the Lord of creation humbled Himself, never asking for fanfare. May we follow His example, willing to relinquish our dignity.

Make me humble, as Christ was, Father.

Become What You Are

★ ★ ★ ★ ★

READ MATTHEW 25:14–30.

It seems like a new smartphone or electronic gadget comes out every other week. Each incarnation features some fascinating upgrade of computing—only to be outdone in a few months by another version with even more bells and whistles.

We too often think that way about ourselves: we figure we need constant upgrades. We say that we'll wait to serve until we're "more prepared," we'll get involved in a church "once we find one that we like," and we'll give to missions "when we have more money."

Don't wait. Serve now. Get involved now. Give now. God has already released the resources for the task. He has given you the gifts you need. Use what you have, and God will take care of the rest.

As you are faithful to become what you are, one day you will hear His precious words: "Well done, my good and faithful servant."

Father, show me how to use what You have entrusted to me.

Come and See!

★ ★ ★ ★ ★

READ MATTHEW 11:28-30.

Once upon a time, people who wanted to cheat others by selling balms and pills that promised much but delivered little traveled alone and moved from place to place to make a dishonest living. Nowadays, they bark at us from the nearest television or Internet banner advertisement. They clamor for our attention: "Come here! You must see this!" Too often people fall for the flashy ads and spend their hard-earned money on empty promises.

Someone else in our world is calling out to us: "Come hither!" But what God promises delivers more than we can imagine. He calls us to bring our burdens to Him so that He can give us rest and peace. He promises to give us life that matters, life that works. He promises to take the bad things and use them for good. He promises to be with us now and forever.

Wonderful, wonderful indeed!

Thank You, Father, for Your promise of rest and fulfillment.

....

....

....

....

....

....

....

....

....

The Joy of Rest

★ ★ ★ ★ ★

READ MARK 1:31–35.

Superheroes never seem to rest. When does Batman get a personal day? Superman's Fortress of Solitude is always a little cluttered—there's no time for cleaning when the world needs to be saved, after all.

Often we think we can live like superheroes. We'll spend the whole week running around, and when we reach the weekend, we stay busy with the tasks that need finishing. Soon enough, our days become joyless because even our "rest"—playing video games or watching television—isn't very restful.

Jesus knew the importance of real rest: rest found in the Father. After a day spent healing the sick and lame, He would retreat to spend time with God. Today, take a few moments in your own Fortress of Solitude with the God who loves you sincerely. There you will find true joy.

I am tiring myself out. Let me rest in You, O God.

Deep Roots

★ ★ ★ ★ ★

READ MATTHEW 4:1-11.

Seeds that blow onto rocky soil rarely find a place to put down deep roots. Without solid grounding and nutrition, seedlings wither or stay small.

People need grounding and nourishment too. Perhaps you've set aside a portion of each day to read, learn, pray, and grow more deeply into the rich and nourishing soil of God's Word. This time you spend with Him is as important as eating and sleeping. When Jesus was tempted by Satan, He demonstrated that we can overcome the tempter's snares by knowing the Scriptures. The psalmist knew it was important to spend time with God, reminding us that His Word will light our way in a dark world (Psalm 119:105).

Going without nourishment or rest for too long makes a person weak. The same is true of one's spiritual life. We keep it strong and healthy by spending time with God.

Thank You for our time together, Lord.

Do You Have the Time?

★ ★ ★ ★

READ EPHESIANS 1:18-20.

Do you want to spend more time with God? Perhaps you want to read your Bible and pray, but you're just too busy.

An old song by Harry Chapin laments how the busyness of a father keeps him from spending time with his son. When the father is older and regretting lost time, he attempts to make up for it by spending time with his adult son. But his son has no time to give. He's simply too busy.

Our heavenly Father is always there for us whenever we call on Him. He's even there watching over us when our lives are so busy we don't have time to think!

Let's make time for God today and every day, spending time with Him in prayer and praise. How sad it would be to come to the end of your life full of regret that you didn't spend more time learning, growing, and sharing God's love.

I want to spend more time with You, Lord.
Help me to make the time each day.

An Undeniable Treasure

★ ★ ★ ★ ★

READ 1 CORINTHIANS 15:20-23.

We tend to think of ourselves as common, run-of-the-mill, average. When we look at the extraordinary gifts and talents of other people, we consider ourselves to be ordinary in comparison. But to God, each of us is exceptional, unequaled, beyond measure.

Because we are specially designed by God, we are incomparable, perfect in every way. God has a special love for each of His sons and daughters, as a father loves his children. Each of us is an undeniable treasure, in a class by ourselves, one-of-a-kind, and loved uniquely by our heavenly Father. And through the sacrifice of His sinless Son, Jesus our Lord, we are a cherished member of God's family, destined to spend eternity with Him in heaven.

Jesus Christ died freely for the church, and He loves each of us as if we were the only person on the planet. His shed blood has removed our imperfections. And though we still sin, when God looks at us now, all that's in view is Jesus.

Lord, help me to never forget what You did for me at Calvary.

Cry Out to God

★ ★ ★ ★ ★

READ PSALM 50:15-17.

Are you experiencing difficulty today? Perhaps you are struggling through a painful situation or bearing the burden for another who is suffering.

The apostle Paul knew hardships firsthand. He was persecuted, beaten, shipwrecked, and imprisoned. He also suffered from a burden so painful that he described it as a "thorn in his flesh." Paul was honest with God, asking Him to take the thorn away. But God reminded him that His grace was all Paul needed (2 Corinthians 12:7–10). His faithfulness is tried and proven.

Whatever difficulty you face today, cry out to God. Pour out your heart to Him in prayer and lay all of your pain at God's feet. His power is perfected in our weakness and His grace is just as sufficient for us today as it was for the apostle Paul.

Lord, I need You now. Bring Your grace and peace
to me in the midst of my pain.

The Reason Is Love

★ ★ ★ ★ ★

READ 1 JOHN 4:7-12.

It's a classic story. Gepetto the woodworker carves a boy out of wood and wishes he would become real. His wish is granted, and Pinocchio is transformed into a real boy with a mind of his own.

Pinocchio's boyish ideas land him in the wrong crowd and he runs away from home. This act of rebellion breaks his father's heart, causing Gepetto to experience the ache of separation between himself and the child he created.

Knowing full well that mankind would make a similar decision to rebel, God created us anyway. He knew our outcome before He formed the dust we were made from, and yet with love immeasurable, He formed us. The human race soon rebelled, but God's love didn't waver.

His love for you doesn't waver either.

Lover of my soul, teach me to love as You love.

Let Go

★ ★ ★ ★ ★

READ EPHESIANS 3:20-21.

Bringing those we love to God in prayer isn't always an easy task. We see a spouse struggling, a child wandering, a friend hurting—and we want to help. It's our first instinct! Yet sometimes their struggle runs so deep that we can only pray, keenly aware that there is nothing more we can do. The person we are praying for may be blind to God's work. Or uninterested in His answers. Or in too much pain to listen. It is in those times that we remind ourselves—minute by minute, if necessary—that God can do far more in a loved one's life through our prayers than we could ever imagine.

Just as we trust God to be at work in our own lives, so we can trust Him to be at work in the lives of those we love. We can make it a daily habit to hand over our loved ones to the Lord in prayer. He will never let go of them. His Word promises.

Help me trust You, Lord, for those I love who are wandering.

God's Perfect Timing

★ ★ ★ ★ ★

READ ECCLESIASTES 3:11.

All good things come to those who wait" is an adage with little charm if you're the one doing the waiting. Waiting demands patience, and patience calls for being still and knowing God as all-wise, trusting His perfect timing.

Our culture today demands instant satisfaction. Instant food. Instant solving of problems. Instant relief of pain. Wise parents do not succumb to a child's "I want it now" tantrums. God is no different.

Whether you are waiting for the weather to change, the flowers to bloom, the toddler to learn to walk, the pain to cease, the hurt to heal, or for God to answer prayer for a loved one, you can trust God's timing and wisdom. He knows the perfect time for all good things to burst forth in bloom.

Lord, give me patience to wait
and to trust Your wisdom while I wait.

Anything but Easy

★ ★ ★ ★ ★

MATTHEW 6:14-15.

In a child's world, arguments over lost or broken toys and even mean looks happen frequently. Before long, kicking and screaming ensue, and everyone ends up in tears. Usually, though, after a time-out, apologies are made and the incident is forgotten.

If only adult issues were that simple to resolve! In the adult world, differing opinions derail office projects and business partnerships. Marriages turn sour over disagreements. Misunderstandings separate families for generations. Spats divide close friends, turning them into adversaries.

Jesus spoke in Matthew 6 about the importance of forgiveness. Not only does a lack of forgiveness affect others, but it also hinders our own spiritual walk. If Christ willingly forgave us despite our many sins—if He could hang on a cross that we nailed Him to and ask God to forgive us—surely we can offer that same grace to others. Love and forgiveness do not wait to be earned.

Jesus, give me the same forgiving attitude You have.

Fountain of Love

★ ★ ★ ★ ★

READ 1 JOHN 4:19.

In Victor Hugo's *Les Miserables*, a priest opens his home to a man named Jean Valjean, giving him food and shelter—only to have Valjean steal a silver plate and cup and run away. When Valjean is caught by the police, they ask the priest to confirm that Valjean stole the items. In a surprising act of grace, the man of God declares they were a gift and asks Valjean why he forgot to take the candlesticks that went with the set. Valjean, staggered by such kindness, is forever changed. And from that day forward, he vows to lead a life of honesty, generosity, and graciousness.

It took only one act of self-sacrificing love to radically alter the life of that criminal. Have you come face-to-face with God's boundless, incomprehensible love? Have you let it change your life?

Lord, I am not worthy of Your limitless love,
but I praise You for it.

Grace in Humility

★ ★ ★ ★ ★

READ MATTHEW 5:3-12.

Living the way Jesus taught is often in direct contrast to the way the world lives. To be poor in spirit means we understand our own helplessness to stand before a holy God. We recognize that we are nothing apart from the grace of Jesus. What a humbling thought!

If we want to experience the joy of living the way God wants us to live, humbling ourselves is a great place to start. This means giving when it's easier to take, assisting when it's easier to be indifferent, loving others when it's easier to ignore them. By being poor in spirit we will be blessed beyond measure and experience God's abiding peace. The rewards might come in this life, and then again, they might not. But God promises that the kingdom of heaven will belong to us.

We find the deepest peace in humbling ourselves and following Jesus.

Jesus, help me to humbly follow You.

Boldness for the Timid

★ ★ ★ ★

READ 2 TIMOTHY 1:6–7.

Psychologists tell us that there are four basic personality types: choleric (excitable), sanguine (confident), phlegmatic (calm), and melancholy (persistent). Depending on your temperament, the thought of being a bold witness for Christ might ignite a fire in your soul or fill you with dread. As Christians we can rest in the knowledge that being a witness for Christ doesn't depend upon our personality but on the Spirit of God working in our lives.

Each of us has spiritual gifts bestowed upon us by our Creator. God created our personalities, and He calls us to be bold witnesses for Him whether we are assertive or timid by nature. Our hope in Christ doesn't spring from our temperament but from our salvation.

Scripture urges us to always be willing to share the hope that is within us, in the ways God has prepared for us.

Lord, thank You for the Spirit of God working in me
that makes me bold for You.

Love Story

★ ★ ★ ★ ★

READ EPHESIANS 5:29-32.

The classic love story has a formula: man meets woman and falls in love. Though the woman's heart may be difficult to win, though her suitor may have to overcome many obstacles to gain her love, we always hope that, in the end, their story culminates in a memorable "happily ever after."

How does the man know he's in love? It's not just that his heart races whenever she walks into the room, or that he gets tongue-tied when he tries to speak to her. He knows he's in love because he would do anything for her. He would gladly give his life for hers, knowing that even though he'd be gone, she'd have another chance at life and happiness.

So, too, with Christ and the church. The church is His beloved, His bride. He didn't just say He'd do anything for her; He actually sacrificed His life, giving everything—all because of love. What a love story that is! And it can be yours.

Christ's deep love for you held Him to the cross, where He died for you.

Jesus, thank You for Your sacrifice and love. I surrender myself to You.

Leave the Future to God

★ ★ ★ ★

READ ISAIAH 44:21-26.

Tarot card readers. Astrologists. Psychics. Fortune-tellers. All claim to foretell the future. And all are frauds!

The Lord warns against these forms of evil. Deuteronomy 18:10–14 admonishes us to avoid such practices and those who practice them. He wants us to trust Him for what lies ahead and rely on no one else.

But before we applaud ourselves for avoiding such evil, 1 Samuel 15:23–26 reminds us that rebellion is as sinful as witchcraft and stubbornness as bad as worshipping idols. We may not be running to palm readers or consulting mediums to see what the future holds. But is our rebellious and stubborn nature keeping us from seeking God's purposes for our lives? What He wants may not be what we had planned, but we can trust His heart and obediently follow Him.

Jesus, help me to trust You alone for my future
and not worry about what lies ahead.

Delighting in God

★ ★ ★ ★ ★

READ PSALM 33.

Christians who serve God out of obligation use words like ought, duty, expected, and necessary. These words aren't necessarily wrong when pertaining to the faith, but those who cite them as primary reasons for following Christ have lost a sense of a loving, personal relationship with their Savior. It is like the lover who knocks on the front door of his love's house on Valentine's Day, and when she answers he holds out a dozen long-stemmed red roses and says in a flat tone, "Here. These are for you. It's my duty." How appealing would those roses be?

When we express our love for Christ out of duty alone, we sound similar: "There. I've read my Bible. It's my spiritual duty." Such obligatory Christianity, when lacking a delight in Christ, can be loveless and stale. But when we truly delight in Him, when we are drawn to Him in joy, imagine the pleasure that brings to God's heart.

O Lord, make my heart glad in You!

Sailing in Storms

★ ★ ★ ★ ★

READ DEUTERONOMY 31:6.

Have you ever had a day when everything fell apart at once? A day when, suddenly, all the careful plans you laid blew up spontaneously?

These days happen to all of us. Everyone who makes plans will someday see them fall apart. In our corrupted, imperfect world, nothing is permanent. Things break. At times it seems Murphy's Law is as reliable as gravity.

In sailing, often the best way to survive an awful storm is to lower the sails and ride it out. The same is true in life. Though it goes against our every instinct, in times of trouble we must lower our sails—whatever we have control over—and ask God to carry us through the storm.

Take heart; God has not left you. He loves you, and He will not let you drown. Remember that when He is at the helm of your life, you can ride along on His grace.

God, it's hard to survive these storms;
I need You to carry me through.

Stooping to Help Us

★ ★ ★ ★ ★

READ PROVERBS 10:22–25.

A shepherd wandering in darkness and danger to find and rescue one little lamb. A father setting aside his dignity and running to welcome home the son who rejected him and squandered his money. The Son of God reaching out to touch the hand of a leper. Jesus noticing and praising the generosity of a poverty-stricken widow.

So many of the images we have of God—in the parables and in the human face of His Son—show God stooping down to our level.

Christ was willing to humble Himself so that He could help those in need. And He continues to reach down to us so we might receive His strength when temptation hits. He is eager to help us. Every time we reach the end of our strength and can't find our way out of difficult circumstances, we need to stop and ask Him for help. He is never too proud to stoop to our level to give us the help we need.

Lord, let me humbly look to You for help
in my time of need.

Broken

★ ★ ★ ★ ★

READ MATTHEW 27:45-54.

Emotional pain so severe it feels as though daggers are ripping through muscle. Anguish that seems to have no end... These can't possibly be things to embrace. When suffering from a broken heart, it feels impossible that any good could possibly come from such bad.

But God offers a salve to our wounded world: His sovereignty.

Kicking and screaming, we reject His calming words in search of explanations and instant relief. Unfazed, the Son wraps His arms around us until, through the slowing tears, we can focus on the hands. The nail-scarred hands that changed the world.

A broken heart is often the first avenue through which the world is changed. Will you dare to find the purpose for yours? Through the broken heart of our heavenly Father and the sacrifice of His Son, the world is free from sin's bondage. Transformation is possible! Restoration can be ours!

Father, please reveal Your purposes for my brokenness.

....

....

....

....

....

....

....

....

Be with God

★ ★ ★ ★

READ PSALM 119:9-16.

Do you read your Bible? Excellent. Knowing God's Word is essential to our growth. As we study and learn the truth of Scripture, our passion for Him will grow strong.

Do you attend a good church? Wonderful. Sermons that point us closer to God help deepen our relationship with Him, and spending time with other believers strengthens our faith.

There is more to the Christian life, though. Being alone with Jesus, whether in direct prayer or quietly listening—privately, away from the noise of this world—is essential to the Christian life. In these solitary moments, we praise Him, thank Him, confess to Him, and tell Him we love Him...when no one else is watching.

Close the door, turn off your cell phone, and be alone with our Lord. He desires to be with you.

Wherever I am, Lord, I know You are with me.

The Meaning of Life

★ ★ ★ ★ ★

READ JOHN 1:1–5; 3:16.

What joy the Creator must have had in creation, the glorious dawn of God's history with us. Jesus was there with God at the very beginning, and all of history looked forward to the day when He would descend to the earth He created in order to save His people from their sin.

Jesus was fully God and fully man. Because He was willing to wrap His divine glory in human flesh, He truly understands the human condition. During His days on earth, He experienced the fullness of humanity—sorrow, joy, temptation, hunger, thirst, delight, pain, laughter, and so much more. And even though we are totally unworthy, He allowed Himself to become the sacrifice to take care of our sins once and for all.

God's story is our story when we choose to accept the gracious gift of Jesus's sacrifice for us. Real meaning in life is found in our Savior.

Thank You, Lord, for bringing true meaning to my life.

....

....

....

....

....

....

....

....

....

Mosaic

★ ★ ★ ★ ★

READ JEREMIAH 29:11–14.

The history of mankind is full of hatred, bigotry, wars, and bloodshed. Collectively, our conscience is stained.

Knowing how dark and shameful our history is, it's difficult to think that anyone is in control of it—much less a benevolent, all-powerful God. Yet Scripture tells us that the book of history is in the hand of God. He has a plan greater than what we can see from our limited perspective. We are like ants crawling around on an enormous mosaic, scoffing, "How on earth could a picture be made of this?" Yet God, who stands outside history, has a purpose.

Despite all our flaws, we can take comfort in the fact that God has a great plan for us, one more intricate and beautiful than we can imagine. We are—we have always been—His passion.

Father, help me to trust You with the plan
You have for Your people.

Resting in God's Best

★ ★ ★ ★ ★

READ JAMES 4:7.

Submission is a four-letter word in our culture. We resist anything or anyone limiting our personal freedoms, and we equate submission with weakness.

But submitting to God's plan for us and, yes, even to His rules in the Bible, doesn't mean that we are weak. On the contrary, Christians are strong—we stand firm in the faith and defend our beliefs while dressed in the full armor of God. Even the most stout-hearted warriors follow the commands of their leader. The Bible teaches that the most courageous thing we can do as soldiers of the Almighty is to submit to the leadership of our Commander in Chief.

The Lord is the foundation of our faith and the source of all meaning. When we follow in His steps and do things God's way instead of our own way, we receive His blessing and peace.

Help me to submit to You, Lord, that I may be happy and blessed.

Anchored

★ ★ ★ ★ ★

READ 2 CORINTHIANS 12:1–1.

A flash of lightning and a clap of thunder announce the beginning of a storm. A boat far from shore drops its anchor and waits. Winds howl; waves roar as the storm intensifies. More clouds roll in. The sky grows darker. The wind and the waves attack the boat, and it rocks back and forth, as if it's about to be torn apart by the elements. But the anchor rests safely beneath the surface, far below the rough waves. It holds the boat in place, stabilizing it in the storm, keeping it secure.

When we face life's storms, however bleak and rocky, we can place our trust in God and make Him our anchor. He has not promised a life free from storms, but He has promised us that He will go with us. So in life's storms, let's cling to the anchor of God's abiding presence to stay afloat and remain secure in Him.

Lord, may I rely on You and remember Your presence.

Bootstraps

★ ★ ★ ★

READ PSALM 44:6–8.

Americans love the idea of self-sufficiency. From the first day at kindergarten to the last overpriced therapy session, we are told over and over that we are "good enough" and that we can do anything if we just "believe in ourselves." Publishers sell millions of self-help books, all of which encourage us to "pick ourselves up by our bootstraps."

But no matter how good these platitudes may sound, they don't reflect reality. Why? Because self-sufficiency is impossible. As much as we hate to admit it, no one can get through life on his or her own strength. At some point, we all need help, and self-help can't cut it.

God knows we can't get by alone. That's why He didn't leave us to pick ourselves up by our bootstraps; He reaches down to help us up.

Lord, thank You for the strength You provide.

His Hands and Feet

★ ★ ★ ★ ★

READ 1 CORINTHIANS 12: 12–27.

Three times in the New Testament the apostle Paul tells believers that we are all a part of the body of Christ. Jesus is not physically walking the earth and preaching today, but through the church, He shares His love and spreads the good news of salvation to the world.

But what if you're not comfortable speaking in front of crowds? Paul makes reference to that in 1 Corinthians 12. Just because you're not a mouth doesn't mean you have nothing to offer as a part of the body of Christ. You might be the hands, preparing a meal for a sick friend. Maybe you're the feet that deliver a meal. Or you might be the eyes that are able to recognize those in need.

As a Christian, you are a part of the body of Christ—and together we are the living, breathing representation of Jesus to our world.

Help me to be a good representative of You
to the world, O Lord.

Going through the Motions

★ ★ ★ ★ ★

READ PSALM 19:1.

The Pharisees of Jesus's time were very good at giving God lip service. They kept the Hebrew laws, they quoted Scripture, and they stood on street corners and prayed. From all outward appearances, the Pharisees were holy.

But Jesus knew their hearts. He saw the blackness that consumed them through their corruption and pride.

What does God see when He searches your heart? Do the words you speak and the prayers you pray accurately depict the meditations of your heart?

God wants our cheerful obedience. He wants us to show love, not just talk about it. He wants us to give generously, not out of compulsion but from a joyful spirit. He desires constant communication rather than a ten-second prayer before each meal. He wants our hearts to yearn for Him, to dwell in His power.

Let's not just go through the motions—let's give God our sincere devotion always.

God, help me to mean every word I pray; be the desire of my heart!

Home Away from Home

★ ★ ★ ★ ★

READ 2 CORINTHIANS 5:1-8.

A popular Christian author wrote a modern-day allegory about the Christian's desire to be close to God. He painted the picture of the believer diving into a pool of God's grace and being joyfully submerged in God's love, emerging cleansed and renewed. He feels completely at home there, never wanting to leave.

We—the creation—long to be with our Creator. We yearn to be with Him in heaven, but for now, we're relegated to this earth.

However, we have the capacity to experience God's presence. He's blessed us with His Word. He's provided family and friends who encourage and love us. We have ministers, Sunday school teachers, and small group leaders who help us grow. We can listen and sing along to countless melodies that praise His name. He hasn't left us to fend for ourselves!

God's presence is in our hearts here, even as we long to be at home with Him.

Lord, thank You for Your presence in my life,
drawing me closer to You.

The Voice of God

★ ★ ★ ★ ★

READ 1 KINGS 19:11–12.

When we pray, we need to be quiet in order to hear the voice of God speaking to us. But how often is God's voice drowned out by the chaos of our busy lives?

God is the most powerful being in the UNIVERSE. When He spoke, our solar system and everything on planet Earth came into being. He breathed and Adam lived. With that much power, imagine what might happen if He were to sing or shout! But the Bible says He speaks to us in a still, small voice.

Maybe the reason we don't hear God's voice when we pray is that we are surrounded by too much noise. Like the music at a concert when we can't hear ourselves think, the cacophony of everyday life can overshadow God's voice—no matter the volume.

It's time to remove the distractions and dial down the chaos, to listen for God's voice beyond the clamor. It will be a welcome sound indeed.

I need to hear You, Lord. Help me to really listen and know Your voice.

Make Your Choice

★ ★ ★ ★ ★

READ JOSHUA 24:15.

We love to sit around with cups of steaming coffee and talk about ideas. How would we solve the budget problems in our country? What's the best way to grill a steak? We express our opinions and walk away changed or unchanged, ready to act or not. It doesn't really matter—we were just discussing ideas.

Many people treat God as if He were just an idea we can discuss and then walk away unchanged. That is precisely why God did not leave us with just a set of ideas; He gave us a person, Himself. He gave us someone to follow rather than an idea to discuss.

Because God gave us a person, that leaves us with a choice. We have to do something about this person. We have to decide whether to believe what God said about Himself or not. We have to choose.

And that choice makes all the difference.

Father, I choose You—today and every day.

God Is

★ ★ ★ ★ ★

READ 1 CORINTHIANS 15:54-58.

God is. His existence is without question. As we accept the reality of a God who is eternally present, our doubts are washed away.

If we examine our fear and break into its core, we will see that every fear is rooted in doubting God's existence—doubting that anyone is out there who can help us. When we know that God is, however, we can be assured that His promises are true. Knowing this, we can live fearlessly.

Because God is, He will be who He is eternally. He will keep His promises—to stay close, to walk with us through the trials, to turn evil to good, and to raise us again at the last day.

Be still and know that God is. And think about what that means to you today.

Quiet my fears, God, because of who You are.

Heaven's Answers

★ ★ ★ ★ ★

READ MATTHEW 6:5-8.

Have you ever thought God wouldn't want to hear about a deep longing of your heart? Have you spent your quiet time talking with God about what you think He wants you to pray, rather than what was really on your mind?

Prayer is one area where we need not hesitate or fear. We can run to God and tell Him what is on our hearts—the need for a job, concerns for a spouse or a child, overcoming health issues and financial struggles.

God longs to hear whatever is troubling us, whatever is occupying our thoughts. And as we come to Him with our problems, requests, and desires, He invites us to lay them at His feet and trust His answers to come in His time, His way.

He knows us far better than we know ourselves. He knows the beginning and end. Let's be open to His answers, for He will respond according to our true needs.

How can we know this for certain? Because He knows and loves us best.

Dear Lord, honest prayer is a gift, and I am grateful for it.

Gentle Persistence

★ ★ ★ ★ ★

READ PSALM 17:1–9.

Have you ever tried to force open a door that was stuck? You pushed until something gave way—either a pulled muscle or a splintered door frame. This is an example of impatience running ahead of wisdom, with disastrous results.

Sometimes we approach prayer the same way we tackle a stubborn door. In our hurry to get through our prayer time, we push and shove. We know exactly what should be done, why it should be done, and how it should be done. And we're not shy about letting our opinions and feelings about the matter be heard!

Effective prayer acknowledges our need for the Master Craftsman instead of trying to force the key in the lock. God wants us to spend time with Him, getting to know Him and being shaped by Him. As you talk to Him today, let your words and attitude be characterized not by demanding insistence but by gentle, humble persistence. We are merely acknowledging that we need Him.

And that is exactly the way He wants it.

Hear my cry, Lord, I need Your help today.

Your Offering

★ ★ ★ ★

READ MATTHEW 6:19-21.

When it's time to collect items to give away or to sell at a garage sale, we think about the things we don't need: that extra coffeemaker someone gave us, that picture frame gathering dust, those books we never read. But we keep a vise grip on the things we think we need the most—the items of most value to us. Ironically, some of those things end up at the next garage sale.

Jesus advised His disciples to let go of the things of this earth and transfer their grip to the things that aren't of this world. The possessions of heaven can't be lost or stolen here on earth. Offering ourselves and our belongings to God is a way of storing up treasure in heaven. It also helps us to hold things loosely in this life. We came into this world with nothing and we can take nothing we have in this world into the next.

What will you offer God?

O Lord, I offer You my life and all that I have.
Use them as You see fit.

I Did It

★ ★ ★ ★ ★

READ 1 SAMUEL 2:1-11.

The lame man could walk. The leper was healed. The shriveled hand was restored. All were miracles accomplished by the power of God. But what if each individual had taken the credit instead?

What if the lame man bragged, "I used to be crippled, but I did a lot of physical training and over time I strengthened my legs so they could move on their own."

"I used to be a leper," another said, "but I cleaned myself constantly and eventually the spots went away."

The man who had a shriveled hand said, "I used to have a deformed hand, but I stretched it and put lotion on it every day for years and it healed."

Sounds ludicrous, doesn't it? Yet it's too easy to take credit for blessings that come from God. Pride tells others that we accomplished the miracles in our lives—whether a healing, a renewed relationship, or some other success—on our own, when the credit belongs to God.

May I always credit You for the good in my life, God.

....
....
....
....
....
....
....
....

Applying the Cross

★ ★ ★ ★

READ MARK 8:34–38.

The notion of leaving a splinter in your finger seems silly. If the splinter is ignored, your finger turns red, and if left long enough it becomes infected. It is as if your body screams, "Get it out of me!" How much more absurd is the notion of embracing a cross. It represents a cruel form of physical torture that causes loss of blood and suffocation. It is as if your body and soul scream, "Get me down from here!"

The cross that God calls us to bear adds nothing to Christ's cross and sacrifice for our sin. But in their various forms—a cross of depression, a cross of a terminal disease, a cross of job loss, or a cross from weariness from life's daily grind—they crucify the self-dominated life. As we apply the cross to our lives and die to ourselves, we begin to live instead to the Spirit, who brings forth the fruit of His character in us.

Lord Jesus Christ, I want to be raised
to fruitful living through Your Spirit.

What Would He Do?

★ ★ ★ ★ ★

READ LUKE 6:27–36.

In the 1990s the question "What would Jesus do?" spread across America as youth groups studied Charles Sheldon's 1896 novel *In His Steps* and wore bracelets with the letters WWJD. This question called believers to ask themselves whether or not they were living as Christ would have them live. It encouraged them to model their lives after Christ's and become walking testimonies of the Savior.

The Lord has called us to be more like Him, to show His love to the unlovable and to reach out to the unreachable. Jesus loved Judas, who betrayed Him, and Pilate, who sent Him to the cross. And He taught His followers to follow His example by loving their enemies and praying for those who persecuted them.

If we truly are to do what Jesus would do, then we will respond to others in love, not hate. We will love others as Jesus Himself loves them.

Lord Jesus, help me to love like You.

Costly Forgiveness

★ ★ ★ ★ ★

READ COLOSSIANS 3:12-15.

The film *The Passion of the Christ* gives viewers a vivid emotional understanding of Christ's suffering for our forgiveness. In the movie, the events of Christ's crucifixion are portrayed in sights and sounds that are almost too much to handle!

Attempt to imagine what it was like for the heavenly Father to put His Son on the cross to suffer and die.

"Stop it!" we might scream from the perspective of our human justice. "Jesus does not deserve to suffer!" Yet for God the Father, that was the point of Calvary. As a sinless man Jesus did not deserve to die, but He willingly took on our sin. He suffered for our forgiveness.

As beneficiaries of His suffering, should we offer anything less to others? Though we will never suffer as Christ did for us, we must accept in our forgiving others that sometimes we too must bear suffering for the sake of love.

Lord, grant me a willingness to suffer in forgiving others.

Fingerprints of God

★ ★ ★ ★ ★

READ GENESIS 1:26-31.

The fingerprints of God are upon every soul. In the Garden of Eden, God scooped up dirt from the ground to form the first man, Adam. Into the man God breathed life and proclaimed it was very good. Every person since has value as God's crowning achievement.

What makes us prized by God ahead of the eagle with its grandeur, the ant with her diligence, the lion with his majesty? The distinction lies with God, who said, "Let us make mankind in our image, in our likeness" (Genesis 1:26). As humans, we have the distinction of being the only beings in all of creation who were made in the image of God.

As ennobling as it is to bear God's likeness, far nobler is having the very Spirit of God dwelling in us. On this side of heaven we are jars of clay dusted with the fingerprints of God as His chosen vessels in Christ, redeemed to display His glory!

May your fingerprints be all over me, Father,
as You shape me into the likeness of Christ.

Jesus, Our Great Reward!

★ ★ ★ ★ ★

READ 1 CORINTHIANS 2:6–13.

Winnie the Pooh, written by A. A. Milne in 1926, is a classic children's story with many lasting lessons. In it we discover a delightful troupe of characters with their own unique personalities: Christopher Robin's kindness, Rabbit's nervousness, Tigger's playfulness, Pooh's curiosity, and Eeyore's sadness. In his perpetual gloom, a gray cloud follows Eeyore, raining down wherever he goes as he sighs, "Woe is me."

Many Christians have an Eeyore-like outlook on life. But Jesus said, "I came that [you] may have life and have it abundantly" (John 10:10 ESV)! If that is Jesus's intent, then as His followers we have the privilege to enter the joy of the Lord faithfully and earnestly.

Jesus Himself is our great reward! What else could we possibly want? Let's wipe off our frowns and choose to live in the joy of the Lord today.

Jesus, I believe that You are my great reward.

One in a Billion

We fight monotony. Some days we feel like we are just a speck on a massive planet filled with billions of specks. How can we possibly matter to God?

Our God, however, must exult in a certain amount of monotony. While we are astounded at the wide variety of flowers all over the globe, we also stand in wonder of a field decorated with millions of daisies. Just one flower, duplicated a million times, yet each was created separately and put into its own special place.

Similarly, we are much like all other humans. We exhibit the same general size, shape, and functions. Yet each of us is created by God, different from the next person and lovingly put into the place that God has specially planned for us. No one on the planet is just like you. You were uniquely designed in your mother's womb. God knows you intimately and intricately.

Monotonous? Boring? Not on your life. You're one in a billion!

Lord, help me to understand Your intimate love for me.

The Specialist

★ ★ ★ ★ ★

READ MARK 9:20-29.

After hours of work and effort, you finally accomplish a seemingly impossible task. With a sigh of relief, you energetically move on to your next task. However, when your plan hits a crater-sized pothole and you end up on the side of the road waiting for a tow truck, quite the opposite happens. Instead of relief and energy, you feel frustration and disappointment.

Are you dreaming of something today that seems out of reach? Do your needs seem impossible for you to meet on your own? Are you facing a challenge that seems unsolvable? Take courage in the fact that God specializes in impossible situations.

When your circumstances seem impossible, don't look down in despair—look up to God and His goodness, graciousness, and mercy as you eagerly wait for His answers and provision. Redemption in Christ is just the beginning of what God has in store for you. Believe God for the impossibilities in life. He is able to handle anything that comes your way.

God, I give my impossible situation to You to handle.

God's Eternal Plan

★ ★ ★ ★ ★

READ EPHESIANS 1:3–14.

Every human heart yearns for a sense of purpose in life. Just below the surface of our consciousness lie such questions as: "Is what I am doing significant?" "Who cares about what I do?" "What really matters in life?"

It might surprise you to learn that Solomon, a man who had achieved astounding success as king of Israel, also struggled with his own significance. Despite all his earthly achievements, he mused, "Vanity of vanities...all is vanity" (Ecclesiastes 12:8 ESV). If a man as wise and wealthy as King Solomon struggled to find purpose in life, where does that leave the rest of us who will never attain such a lavish existence?

We can trust in God's Word, which says that we do have a purpose. According to God's eternal plan, He predestined us for adoption as His sons and daughters through Jesus Christ. He designed each of us with a unique purpose—to love Him and serve Him.

God, help me to see Your eternal design in the details of my life.

Taking a Backseat Willingly

★ ★ ★ ★ ★

READ MATTHEW 20:20-28.

An elderly mother is in need of care and supervision. But her children are too busy with their own lives. They argue over who should take care of her. "You live closer to her." "But you have more time." And on and on it goes. The mother goes without the care she needs, and the siblings get cross with each other.

Another elderly mother is also in need of care. But her children willingly come to her aid and provide what she needs. They are grateful for the chance to care for their mom, even though it may be inconvenient. And the family grows closer together as they express love for one another.

There's quite a difference between those who carry their crosses willingly and those who do not, or who do so begrudgingly.

Maybe we all need a reminder about the first being last and the last being first in God's kingdom. Each of us has burdens to bear. No one is immune from suffering. May we love one another and finish strong. That will honor our Savior.

Lord, move me to serve You willingly.

More Human

★ ★ ★ ★ ★

READ JOHN 14:15-31.

This side of heaven, Christians do not live perfectly. Yet all Christians do have a perfect standing before God, having received "the righteousness of God through faith in Jesus Christ" (Romans 3:22 ESV).

Our position in Christ, however, does not always mean we live like Christ. We are still very human with all our foibles, fears, and sinful desires. When a church-goer acts less than saintly, those outside the church cry, "The church is a bunch of hypocrites!" Certainly Christians sometimes fail to live up to their name.

We do not deny that we are still human and can sin like the rest of humanity. What makes us different is the presence of One in us who transforms us desire by desire, attitude by attitude, and action by action. Through Him we become more human as we become more like Christ in our thoughts, actions, and lives.

Jesus, may the words of my mouth and the attitudes
of my heart reflect Your presence in me.

Doing Little Things

★ ★ ★ ★ ★

READ LUKE 16:10.

Have you ever heard someone say, "I want to be second place"? How about, "I'd like to get straight Bs on my report card," or "I plan to own a string of second-rate restaurants"? Sounds silly, doesn't it?

No matter how small or seemingly insignificant the task God is asking you to do, it is something He designed you to do for the body of Christ. Maybe God hasn't designed you to be a world-renowned preacher or famous missionary. Maybe inviting your neighbors to dinner, working on the assembly line, or serving in the church nursery is the very thing God wants you to do. Are you willing to do those little things, and nothing more, if that is God's will?

Even a little cricket's chirping can be heard from a great distance. Let's be faithful to do the little things cheerfully and God will be glorified.

Help me to be satisfied in doing the little things for You, Lord.

Our Wild Longings

★ ★ ★ ★ ★

READ EPHESIANS 2:14–18.

What is the deepest longing of your heart? We often pursue that for which we long. C. S. Lewis, author of the children's series the Chronicles of Narnia, is well known for his use of the German word *sehnsucht*, which means "longing" or "intensely missing." This deep longing moves us when we see a beautiful sunset, hear a masterful symphony, or feel a baby's small hand wrap around our finger. God placed this longing within us, and this desire can be satisfied by nothing and no one besides Him. No matter how intensely we pursue other people, places, and things, we "intensely miss" the author of all: God.

The wild longing we all experience will be finally fulfilled when we reach heaven. The most beautiful sunset or symphony is only a shadow of the glory that is to come and the One with whom we will spend eternity.

Filled with longing? Turn to the One who desires to take His place on the throne of your life.

I long for You, Lord.

Accept His Hope

★ ★ ★ ★ ★

READ PSALM 29:10–11.

Ever wish you could find a restart button to push when life gets messy? That frustrating job. That complicated friendship. That circumstance that seems to get more and more untidy the more you try to fix it. Sometimes our difficult situations can feel like a skein of yarn that keeps getting more and more tangled as we work through the knots.

In the midst of the mess, it's easy to forget that God promises to bless His people with victory and peace. He invites us to take our messes to His cross and leave them there, instead of making them our focus. The cross is a restart button. Even when our difficult situation wildly beckons us and ignites our worry, we can choose to believe that God is still in control and He can bless our messes.

Choose to take Him at His word. Give Him your doubts and your fears. Accept His hope.

Help me stand strong and firm on Your promises, Lord.

Who Me, Worry?

★ ★ ★ ★ ★

READ PHILIPPIANS 4:6–9.

When we face difficult circumstances, it's much easier to be anxious than to hand our worries over to God. Instead of letting go of our troubles, we desperately want to hold on to them—ignoring the amazing offer from the Creator of the universe to take our burdens. We seem to be hardwired to rely on ourselves first and God second—or in some cases, not at all.

In times of difficulty and uncertainty, we should pray and let God do the worrying. This means the next time we are tempted to fret about our finances or relationships, our health or loved ones' safety, our job or anything else, we should let the Lord handle it—and step out of the way. It won't be easy at first. Old habits die hard. But if we are to truly live out our faith and experience other-worldly peace, we find the answer in giving our worries to God and trusting Him to work out all things for our good and for His glory.

God, help me to pray and leave the leave my worries with You.

Chasing Perfection

★ ★ ★ ★ ★

READ HEBREWS 2:14-18.

At the Montreal Olympics in 1976, Romanian gymnast Nadia Comaneci became the first gymnast to be awarded the score of a perfect ten. The whole world watched, breathless, as her routine on the uneven bars earned her a place in history. At the tender age of fourteen, Nadia set the bar high for those who strived for a perfect score.

Countless gymnasts and other athletes who make perfection their goal toil endlessly hour after hour, day after day, year after year. And chasing after perfection isn't limited to athletes. Believers who become ensnared in the chase begin to see only the goal instead of the God behind it. And thus is legalism born.

God gives us rest from the chase with the promise that someday we will reach perfection by His grace. For now, He helps us in our imperfection. He forgives us when we give in to temptation and fall far short of the mark. He takes pity on us and helps us in our weaknesses. Chasing perfection? Pursue the perfect God.

God, may my chase for perfection lead to You.

Risky Business

★ ★ ★ ★ ★

READ 2 CORINTHIANS 4:7-15.

What do we seek most in life? Most of us want to do well—and there's certainly nothing wrong with education and honorable service and quality work and receiving kudos for those things. Few of us, however, are out trying to get scars.

This is not a call to jump into an extreme sport that's sure to give physical scars. But it is a call to do something risky. It's a call to do the things that will bring glory to God, regardless of how much they might hurt.

Far too often, safety sits at the top of our priority list and hides God's agenda for our lives. God is looking for people who are willing to live dangerously and be risk takers for the honor and glory of His name.

In the end, He'll be looking for scars that show we have taken the risk to sacrifice ourselves in service to Him. What will He see on us?

Father, I am willing to receive scars if they bring You glory.

Unchanging

★ ★ ★ ★ ★

READ HEBREWS 13:8.

Life is filled with times of transition and change. The celebration of a wedding is followed by the adjustment into a new home, a new family, and a new name. The joy a mother experiences as she watches her young child proudly head off to kindergarten is mixed with the bittersweet feelings of change.

It is possible to have peace amid all the transitions of life because our heavenly Father never varies. Situations and people around us change, but God never changes.

Our heavenly Father is unshakable and unchangeable. Scripture assures us that God is immutable—He is the same yesterday, today, and tomorrow. He is the solid rock we can rest against. And when we reflect on His unchanging nature, we can find stability. As we lean on Him, the tension in our shoulders dissipates. Our muscles relax. We find peace.

Whatever changes you're facing, lean on God. Peace is waiting.

Thank You, Father, for Your peace.

God in Our Weakness

★ ★ ★ ★ ★

READ 2 CORINTHIANS 12:9–10.

Sometimes it feels like we're not strong in Christ at all. We falter. We trip. We try and fail. We serve to the point of exhaustion. How can we possibly be of any value to God and His kingdom?

Oddly enough, it is in our weaknesses that God works in us the most. His strength gives us power even when we don't realize it. The weaker we feel, the more of God we bring to the situation. This is when we make the strongest impressions on others. We fade into the background as God's presence and glory are revealed through our weaknesses. We become the strongest of examples for Him when we least know it.

In those weak moments, we sow seeds of faith. Under God's watchful eyes, those little seeds, sown in the dust of our daily lives, will blossom into immortal flowers of eternal life.

Keep planting. God will tend the garden and produce the growth.

Work especially in my weakness, Lord.

Radical

★ ★ ★ ★

READ PSALM 82:2–4.

Many celebrities are known by their causes. Benefits are hosted for victims of AIDS, earthquakes, floods, and a variety of diseases. Raising money for the plight of the helpless is in vogue.

Jesus had a soft spot for the poor and needy too. But He did much more than host a benefit concert or raise money. He got eyeball-to-eyeball with them and their suffering. He touched the leper, healed the blind, and spoke with the widow, the adulterous woman, and the Samaritan at the well. His approach was unpopular. It was scandalous. It was radical.

Jesus calls us to follow His example to help the poor and defend the defenseless. Will you adopt an orphan or befriend a homeless person? Will you clean up after disasters or volunteer in a soup kitchen, food pantry, or shelter? Raising money helps, but it is only when we get personal, when we look into their eyes and touch them, that we love the poor the way Jesus loves them. And that's radical.

God, help me get personal in helping the poor and defending the defenseless.

The Problem of Pain

⋆ ⋆ ⋆ ⋆ ⋆

READ JOHN 16:25-33.

People seek pain relief in many forms today: aspirin, ibuprofen, prescription muscle relaxers. And those are just for physical pain. To alleviate emotional pain, some try to medicate themselves in other ways: alcohol, legal and illegal drugs, work, relationships, hours spent trolling the Internet. Still the pain lingers like an unwanted guest. But pain is usually the symptom of an underlying problem. Unless the problem is dealt with, the symptom of pain will remain.

Jesus assured His disciples that they would face the pain of persecution and suffering—symptoms of living in a fallen world. But He also gave them some good news: Jesus never met a problem He couldn't overcome. Yes, His followers would go through deep waters. But they would not be alone and defenseless. Jesus would be with them.

None of us will pass through this life pain free. But the ultimate pain reliever still is, and always will be, Jesus.

Jesus, I offer You the pain I feel and accept the peace of Your presence.

Toss that Mountain

★ ★ ★ ★ ★

READ MARK 11:22-25.

Mountains can be a beautiful sight when they're stretching over the horizon in all of their majesty. But when the only mountain you see is a problem you can't solve, words like impossible come to mind, not beautiful. In the face of such a seemingly insurmountable situation, you consult your resources—only to find that they are dwarfed in comparison. What will you do?

If you're facing a mountain-sized problem, Jesus invites you to give that mountain a toss. Impossible, you say? Not for God. Moving mountains is His specialty. All He requires from us is trust. Trust in God is the great mountain mover. When we believe that He has our best interests at heart and delights to hear from His children, we can pray with confidence that God will answer and provide everything we need.

Why not exchange your doubt for the rest that trusting God provides?

I want to trust You, Lord. Here are my doubts.
Please provide what I need.

No Option

★ ★ ★ ★ ★

READ ISAIAH 50:4-5.

If we want to follow Christ, we recognize that making Jesus Lord of our lives isn't optional. He doesn't want to wait on the sidelines of our lives, tossing in a little grace here and there while we try to decide if we're going to be totally devoted to Him. As disciples of Jesus Christ, we are already on His team. We are committed, and that commitment means accepting His lordship over our lives.

Lordship means that Jesus is the center of our lives—not an extra thrown in, mixed with all of our other priorities and focuses and desires. As the King of kings and Lord of lords, Christ is over all and in all and through all. He is the very reason for our existence.

Lordship means that our lives revolve around Him in every decision, every word, and every step.

Lordship means that we walk with Him every step of the way.

Lordship means we are His and He is ours—totally and completely.

Jesus, be Lord over every part of my life.

The Fairy-Tale Life

★ ★ ★ ★ ★

READ PSALM 139:13-18.

As children, we were delighted to read fairy tales and dreamed that once upon a time we, too, would fall in love with a princess or Prince Charming and live happily ever after. But as we grew older, we realized that real life seldom has a fairy-tale ending.

We only need to scan the headlines to realize all the disappointments, from failed celebrity relationships to scandals that cause millionaires to lose their castles. But those who let the Lord write their story find that He composes one that is redemptive and eternal.

Each person is unique and valuable to God. If you honor Him for what you've been given, whether it's much or little, you may still experience troubles in this world. But if you've trusted Christ as Savior, your tale is guaranteed to end well—if not in this life, then in the next, where everything is perfect forever.

Jesus, I trust You with the story of my life and look forward
to my happily ever after with You!

I Love You

★ ★ ★ ★ ★

READ LUKE 23:27–38.

A Jew enduring torture during the Holocaust looks up at her torturer and says, "I love you." A POW in Vietnam raises his bleeding head and tells his tormentor, "I love you." A person walking through the wrong neighborhood says, "I love you," to the gangster whose gun is against his head.

"I love you." These are not words typically spoken to try to change an adversary's mind. These are words of honesty and truth, used to express what is in a loving person's heart. But these three words gain even more profundity when uttered in perilous situations to one's enemies.

How is it possible to love someone who causes so much pain? How could we possibly love our enemies? Ask God, because that's the way He loves us. While we were still God's enemies, He loved us enough to send His Son to die on the cross in our place. And He continues to demonstrate His love for us today.

I hope I never stop wondering at Your love for me, precious God.

Becoming More Like Christ

★ ★ ★ ★ ★

READ ROMANS 8:1-4.

Most of us can remember the day or even the hour we accepted Christ as Savior. Regardless of the details surrounding our conversion, it was a wonderful experience when our sins were forgiven and our eternal home was determined.

But Christ's death and resurrection did more for us than just spare us from eternal damnation; His saving power is also alive and at work in our daily lives. While we were yet dead in our sins, we could not experience the freedom that life in Christ provides. This freedom gives us victory over our sin and the ability—through the Holy Spirit—to daily live in communion with our heavenly Father.

This freedom also prepares us for an ever deeper relationship with Jesus, a relationship that daily draws us closer to Him and changes our desires and objectives to align with His.

May we never lose sight of the journey of freedom and faith that follows salvation.

Daily draw me closer to You and make my desires Yours.

The Firm Peace of God

★ ★ ★ ★ ★

READ PHILIPPIANS 4:4.

Suffering can make the world feel like an unstable place. In the midst of suffering, what we thought was a solid foundation beneath us turns to sand. During those dark times, our faith may be tested. We discover whether the peace of God is truly in our hearts, for that peace will show itself even in the midst of dire suffering.

We have a choice about how we will undergo these trials. When we are filled with God's peace, we can view our suffering with a calm and understanding spirit. We still suffer, but the peace of God that "surpasses all understanding" (Philippians 4:7 NKJV) will help restore our sense of stability. When we turn to God in times of great suffering, His peace will be our comfort.

In our suffering, we find God's peace. Without Him we would be lost; with Him we are forever found.

Thank You for calling me, God, so I might trust in You.

Unity in the Body

★ ★ ★ ★

READ ROMANS 12:4-8.

A tornado ripped through an Oklahoma town in the fall of 2010 and left nothing standing. Debris covered the ground, power lines were down, and buildings lay flattened. One of the most unrecognizable buildings was the community chapel. The residents were devastated by the damage done to their beloved house of worship. Its beautiful stained-glass windows were shattered, and the pews where they had sat, cried, and prayed were now reduced to splinters.

Too often we think of the church as a building, and we confine God to that structure. But the church is more than drywall, carpet, and electrical wires. The church is the body of Christ, and we are all members of it. We are the church, and come what may—wars, famine, even tornadoes—God will reside in us.

Thank You, God, for my fellow church members.
My spiritual family.

Duty Calls

★ ★ ★ ★ ★

READ PSALM 100.

What do you think of when you think of your "duty" to God? Some equate duty with a long, religious to-do list that gives them little joy. This to-do list mentality hinders their relationship with Christ and wearies them with marching orders that contain words like *should* and *ought*. I should love others. I ought to praise God.

Yet a fuller realization of God's goodness and mercy will automatically bring praise and thanks to our lips. It takes the burden out of ministry and sees every act of service as a love offering to our gracious God. In the way that a sparkle in the eyes and a smile on the lips are signs of being in love, our joyful praise of our Savior demonstrates our love for Him.

Have we fully accepted the fact that we are beloved of God? We can drink deeply at the well of His presence and hear the words of praise and thanks fill up our hearts and overflow into our lives of service to God.

Lord, may I always praise You, heart and soul.

What Does God Want?

★ ★ ★ ★ ★

READ MICAH 6:6–8.

Most families, schools, places of employment, and neighborhoods have rules or expectations of behavior. The wise person learns what is required of him or her in order to be a successful participant. When a group's rules are unspoken, however, frustration can quickly set in as those new to the group try to meet expectations they can only guess at.

Have you ever asked yourself what God wants from you? Some believers fear that God has unspoken requirements they can't meet. They consult self-help books or the advice of other believers, all the while fearing God's anger if they get His requirements "wrong."

But God doesn't leave us to wonder what His expectations are; He tells us clearly in His Word. So what does God require? Sincere gratitude and worship. We don't need special skills to tell God thanks. We just need to be willing to spend time with the Father who loves us!

Jesus, I praise and thank You today.

Relying Only on God

★ ★ ★ ★ ★

READ MARK 1:32–35.

Finding peace is increasingly difficult in our technological and informational world. No matter where we go, it's difficult to completely escape mobile phones, the Internet, television, or a hundred other things that vie for our attention. Yet maybe that's the reason we need to seek solitude today more than ever.

We read of Christians many centuries ago who went out to the desert for long periods of time to be alone with God. We also hear about modern-day Christians who take retreats of solitude—for a day, a weekend, or a week—to seek God and His will for their lives.

No matter the length of time, it's important for us to limit the world's hold on us and increase the hold God has on us. There is hardly a better way than to spend time alone—without any distractions—with the Creator of all things.

When we escape from the noise of the world to spend solitary time with God, we will emerge refreshed, rejuvenated, and closer to God.

Teach me to spend time alone with You, please, God.

Go Ahead and Ask

★ ★ ★ ★ ★

READ MATTHEW 7:7-11.

We may think we've hit the prayer lottery when we consider these words of Jesus: "Ask, and it will be given to you" (Matthew 7:7 NKJV). Like a kid in a candy store, we might eagerly ask for this, this, this, and some of this. After all, we have a green light, thanks to the Savior and the knowledge that God delights in His children's prayers.

Yet God reserves the right to answer prayer however He pleases. He does not always say yes to our requests. He's best pleased when His people persist in prayer, rather than insist on a certain answer.

Prayer is an open door to God's ear and heart. Neither is ever closed to His child's softest plea or grimace of pain. No need is considered too great or too insignificant. So, go ahead and ask and keep on asking. According to God's purpose and time frame, He will answer.

Lord God, thank You for giving me the freedom to always come before You in prayer.

Richer and Deeper

★ ★ ★ ★ ★

READ PSALM 76:4-9.

One of the hardest parts of reading is diving deeper into the text. Literature classes are difficult for most students because they're prone to skim over the material. That's why professors push their students to evaluate every word, sentence, and paragraph. It's the only way to find the symbolism and discern the author's intent.

Though God is richer and deeper than any text will ever be, we are too often content with complacency in our relationship with Him. God, the Creator of the universe and the Lover of our souls, is yearning for us to shed our ambivalence—to give up the obligatory gestures and enter into an intimate relationship with Him. From that vantage point, we will be so invigorated that we won't be able to keep ourselves from worshiping Him.

Free me from complacency, Lord; I want something deeper.

Praying God's Heart

★ ★ ★ ★ ★

READ HEBREWS 10:19-23.

Have you ever noticed an elderly couple that bears an uncanny resemblance to each other? They may mirror each other's expressions and mannerisms. It is said that the more time two people spend together, the more they look alike.

The same is true with God. The more time we spend in His Word, the more His words echo from our tongues. The more we invest in prayer, the more His thoughts reverberate within our hearts.

We know that God can be trusted to keep His promises, so we enter boldly into His presence in prayer. We present our requests, not like slaves or servants trembling before a harsh ruler but as dearly loved children approaching a gracious Father. We trust that God knows what we need. We believe that when our hearts seek His will, He will answer. We know that He is good and faithful to guide our prayers until they become His very promises breathed out through us.

God, let my thoughts be Yours, my prayers aligned with Your will.

Knowing You

★ ★ ★ ★ ★

READ PSALM 42:1-2.

It can be intimidating to realize that someone knows a lot about us, at least until we understand the person's motives and how much he or she cares for us. But when it comes to God the Father, we can take comfort in the fact that He knows all about us. We can rest comfortably in His sovereign knowledge because He knit us together in the womb according to His unique design. We need not fear God's intimate knowledge of us, for we know His motives and His love for us.

Nevertheless, God doesn't want this to be a one-way relationship. He offers us the chance to get to know Him too. We can never know Him as well as He knows us, but He longs to enter into a deep and intimate relationship with each of us. He wants us to know Him so well that we easily recognize His heart and His will.

Knowing God, understanding His love for others, and contemplating His desire for justice are things we can experience by deepening our relationship with the Father.

Help me to know You and love You more, dear Lord.

More Like Him

★ ★ ★ ★ ★

READ LUKE 12:22-34.

We all know people who seem to be always in motion, always working, always in the midst of some new project or endeavor. Most of us consider them to be successful. After all, our society admires and esteems busy people.

Yet in our spiritual lives, we are given a completely different model. God's model for success is not so much focused on movement as it is on attitude. The movement of obedience will come later, but first we must make sure our attitudes—our hearts—are in the right place.

If we want to draw closer to God and His will for our lives, we pause to make time for Him and determine His heart for us. We cannot do this while we are constantly in motion; we can only do this by slowing down through prayer, meditation, Scripture reading, and an earnest desire to become more like Him.

Lord, create in me a desire to learn and know Your heart.

A Long Commitment

★ ★ ★ ★ ★

READ 1 PETER 4:12-19.

Life is temporal and fleeting. Considering the history of humankind, we are but a mere speck. Many spend their allotted years chasing after physical pleasures and accomplishments that neither satisfy nor leave a lasting mark.

Yet those who have faith in Christ are blessed, for we are promised eternal life. More than that, we are also promised that we will experience the presence of Christ in our daily lives. As we continue to seek Him, He will reveal more and more of Himself to us. And if we commit ourselves to Him and His work, He will ensure that our labor on this earth is not in vain.

So let us throw off whatever sins, habits, or other earthly barriers constrain us and attach ourselves completely to Christ's presence. Let us seek His vision for our lives, filled with love for our neighbors, service to our fellow man, and allegiance to whatever Christ lays on our hearts.

May His presence be the sole focus of the remaining days we walk the earth.

Lord, fill me with a commitment to serve You with all I have.

A Protected Heart

★ ★ ★ ★ ★

READ HEBREWS 12:28.

How difficult it is to be grateful in our daily lives. We are constantly making comparisons. We compare our children with others', hoping ours are the smartest and the strongest. We compare our talents and our possessions. But comparison is a dangerous game. Sadly, we often come up on the short end—the losing side—and it breeds resentment and gloom.

God never intended for us to compare ourselves or our stuff with others. Instead, He commanded us to look to Him—the giver of life, hope, peace, love, security. Understanding His gifts causes our hearts to well up with gratitude. He gives so much; we deserve so little. Only in acknowledging the Giver, appreciating His unwarranted, incomparable, and unmerited gifts, will our hearts be safe from bitterness and depression.

Lord, my heart wells up with gratitude for all that You have given to me.

A Gift

★ ★ ★ ★ ★

READ EPHESIANS 2:1-10.

A friend holds a package out to you. The paper covering it is stained and crumpled, but your friend assures you that what's inside is beautiful and life-changing. What do you do? Do you trust your friend and open the gift despite its package, or do you turn away in disgust and exclaim, "I don't care what you say; I'm not opening that ugly gift"?

It's amazing that God would give us—the undeserving—new life through the torment of His Son on the cross. The fact that He would take something as ugly as crucifixion and make it beautiful causes us to wonder.

And even more wondrous, God does the same with us. He takes our ugly, sin-stained lives and regenerates them with the purity of His Holy Spirit. He offers us a life-changing package that could be wrapped only one way: the blood of Christ. Only by opening this gift will we receive new life from Christ.

Lord, thank You for Your gift of new life in Your son.

....

....

....

....

....

....

....

....

....

Endless Possibilities

★ ★ ★ ★ ★

READ MARK 10:23-27.

Who then can be saved?" the disciples once asked Jesus. In response, Jesus reminded them of the truth that still stands today: "With men this is impossible, but with God all things are possible" (Matthew 19:25–26 NKJV).

No matter how hard we try, we cannot save ourselves. Left to our own devices, we will fail every time. God tells us to have faith, but we doubt. God says to believe, yet we question. God commands us to trust, but still we hesitate. God understands our limitations, so He grants us the faith. He supplies the belief. He earns our trust.

How amazing that not only does God tell us the qualities He wants us to possess, but then He places the seeds of those traits within our hearts and waters them. He knows our weaknesses and gives us everything we lack. We need not do anything on our own. We are fully supplied for every decision, every journey, and every task by the One who has no limits.

Thank You, God, for equipping me today.

He Rules the World

★ ★ ★ ★ ★

READ ROMANS 1:18–20.

In this modern age, we sometimes forget how dependent we are on life's basic necessities. No matter how advanced our technology or how cutting-edge our modern scientific breakthroughs, we still need air to breathe. We still need water and food to survive. And we still depend completely on our planet, which is perfectly situated within our galaxy to sustain life. Without any one of these, we would be doomed.

When we realize that God is completely in control of all of the details of creation, we are even more astounded at who He is. As we realize the limitlessness of His power and sovereignty, we fall on our knees and worship Him.

As we contemplate who God is and all that He has in His power, we can't help responding to Him in unrestrained devotion and obedience. We serve an incredible, powerful, and majestic God!

Father, help me never to forget just how wonderful and powerful You are.

Lord above All

★ ★ ★ ★ ★

READ PSALM 34:11–16.

When we obey God, we sometimes feel strong enough to take on any opposition. However, how do we feel when we humbly obey, only to see evil continue to get the upper hand? What happens when, even with all of our obedience, things don't quite turn out as planned? Did we mess up? Did we misread God? We might even be tempted to doubt if obedience was worth it.

We must never forget that we are in a spiritual battle. Our obedience naturally stirs up the world of evil; our enemy seeks to discourage us and make us doubt our God. Instead of doubting, remember that in obedience is strength. When we obey God, when we put our faith and trust in Him, He imbues us with such power that evil has no hope of ruling over us. Our strength may falter and fail at times, but the strength of the Lord is everlasting. He is Lord above all, including evil.

God, let my obedience spur the gift of Your might in my life.

Unmerited Grace

★ ★ ★ ★ ★

READ JOHN 1:15-17.

Grace is a magnificent concept that is particularly meaningful to those who follow Christ. Because of grace, our fallen nature and sinful behavior no longer form a barrier between us and God. He bestows His grace upon us without merit—meaning we don't deserve it and can't do anything to attain it.

Yet God's grace is offered to us free of charge. All we have to do is ask for it. His grace is available to us when we are not yet believers in Christ but ask earnestly for Him to enter our hearts, and it's available to us each time we fail but honestly seek His forgiveness. And God's grace never runs out. We can never approach God for grace and hear Him answer, "Sorry, but you have used up your allotment of grace." He continually offers us His abundant, overflowing, undeserved, amazing grace.

Let's live in light of the freeing power of God's unmerited grace in our lives.

Dear God, may I understand Your grace and live purposely,
knowing its power in my life.

Who Am I Now?

★ ★ ★ ★ ★

READ 1 THESSALONIANS 5:23–24.

It's interesting to look back on our lives and review certain decisions and behaviors from the viewpoint of maturity. As we grow older, we gain insights and experience that help us make better decisions.

The same applies to the Christian life—only more so. We all remember the person we were when we were new in Christ: our struggles, the sins we wrestled with, the truths we tried to apply to our lives. Yet as we grow in our faith, we notice that we are less like the person we used to be and more like the person we want to become. We're not quite there yet, but we can thank God for bringing us this far.

God didn't give up on us when we were lost in our sin, He didn't become frustrated with us when as new believers our growth was slow, and He still doesn't walk away from us when as more mature believers we still struggle. We can thank God for His presence through it all.

Father, thank You for working to make me
more like Your Son day after day.

Living in the Present

★ ★ ★ ★ ★

READ JOHN 8:57-58.

When we read the Bible, we sometimes get caught up in the historical facts presented in God's Word. The Old Testament is filled with dramatic events that happened thousands of years ago. Likewise, the New Testament recounts many details about the ministry of Jesus and the formation of the early church, events that occurred in history two thousand years ago.

Yet God is not just the God of the past or the God of a certain historical period. He is the God of the past, present, and future. His power, guidance, and redemptive plan are current and ongoing.

In the Old Testament, God told Moses to tell the Israelites that "I AM" sent Moses to them. In the New Testament, Jesus told those gathered around him "before Abraham was born, I am!"

God does not exist in some past historical context; He exists eternally, eager to interact with us and to be present with us.

Enable me, Father, to see You as the God of the here and now.

Knowing Our Potential

★ ★ ★ ★ ★

READ 1 CORINTHIANS 10:31–33.

We accomplish countless goals in our lives. Whether we sing, write, paint, play a sport, work with numbers, teach, or play a musical instrument, we have reason to thank God daily for the abilities He has given us, for we realize that who we are is God's gift to us.

What we do with these gifts from God is our gift back to Him. Will we use our abilities selfishly, seeking to enrich ourselves or to take advantage of others? Or will we humbly use our gifts to bring glory to our God?

When God formed each of us, He created us with a purpose in mind. We can trust that God knew our potential, even before the moment of our conception, so we can use what we are to give Him glory. There is no greater gift we can give God than becoming what He always meant for us to be.

My gifts are Yours, Lord. Use me to glorify Your name.

The Affair

★ ★ ★ ★ ★

READ ROMANS 6:1–14.

In a popular romance novel, a bride is caught with her former boyfriend the night before her wedding. She had left him and the pain he'd caused her for the prospective groom, who loved and protected her. Her life had improved marvelously, yet despite her fiancé's love, she'd returned to her former sweetheart. His lies possessed her mind, telling her that he was the one she loved, that he was better for her than the groom. She ran back to her ex-boyfriend, even though he had made her feel betrayed and worthless. Readers turn the pages faster and faster, eager to discover if the girl will come to her senses and return to the one who truly loves her.

In like manner, we too often return to the very sins Jesus saved us from. Yet even when we betray Him, He takes us back in His arms, loves and forgives us, and enables us to be who He created us to be. Our relationship with Jesus is a love story that has a happy ending.

Lord, increase my love and faithfulness to You. I love You.

Take and Eat

★ ★ ★ ★ ★

READ PSALM 119:97–104.

At times God seems so mysterious, but He has revealed more of His thoughts to us than we may realize. He imagined the entire universe and crafted the creation to give evidence to His character. We catch a glimpse of God's thoughts every day when we look out our window or in the mirror. More importantly, though, God has given us the ability to know His thoughts through His written Word, the Bible.

The Bible is an invaluable resource. It takes us beyond creation and science to the concept of who we are in relation to God. In the pages of Scripture, God has made Himself an open book in which He tells us of His love, His desires for us, and His plans for the future. He loves revealing Himself to us and is never happier than when we seek Him.

Open the book. Read it with reverence and care. Taste it. Digest it. It is food for your soul.

Lord, speak to me as I read Your precious Word today.

Which Yoke?

★ ★ ★ ★ ★

READ HOSEA 11:1-4.

We like to do things our own way and often bristle when we are told what to do. The Israelites, too, resisted God's commands and often turned from the laws of the Lord. But instead of finding liberation, they merely exchanged one set of regulations for another. They ran from the boundaries of God and His love to become slaves to this world.

Jesus tells us to take up His yoke and find rest. Does that sound strange? Jesus knows what we might refuse to admit—a yoke is not a device of torture but an implement necessary to do a job effectively and efficiently. A yoke distributes force, enabling more work to be done with less effort. A yoke joins a pair and keeps them together so the row is plowed straight. Jesus says to us, "Join My team. We have work to do, and if you stick with Me, you will go faster, farther."

His yoke is easy and His burden is light. He leads us with ropes of kindness and love.

Today I choose Your yoke over the heavy burdens of this world, Lord.

....
....
....
....
....
....
....
....

Finding Joy

★ ★ ★ ★ ★

READ HEBREWS 12:1–2.

Sometimes pain is necessary in order to bring about health. Healing may require surgery to remove an ailment or to reset a broken bone. When we're in the operating room, our wounds are tender and we often cannot see anything good—but it is in those very wounds that joy can settle.

God wants the very best for us. He works in all of His people's lives to create beauty instead of ashes (Isaiah 61:3) and to restore us to spiritual health so that we might glorify Him. He takes our pain and gives us joy.

Every little step of trust and faith that we take—even when we are wounded in life's battles, even when we're in pain—is a step that pushes back the darkness and confusion Satan uses to overwhelm us. Each step of faith says to God, "I hurt, but I trust You."

Then joy has a soft place to settle.

In the midst of life's wounds, dear Lord, give me joy!

When Life Isn't Fair

★ ★ ★ ★

READ MATTHEW 18:21-35.

When we hear of such human atrocities as death camps at Auschwitz, the killing fields of Cambodia, or tribal cleansing in Rwanda, we see the fragility of human justice in an evil world. On a much smaller scale, perhaps someone takes your parking place, a colleague gets the accolades for your hard work, or your life savings are cut in half by a recession. Or maybe you've been devastated by a spouse's betrayal or physically injured by violent crime.

When we encounter circumstances like these, we cry, "It's not fair!" We feel that we have a right to be treated fairly, and we are often angered by the injustice in this world.

In some way, at some level, when we are treated unfairly we need to make the same decision as those who suffer human atrocities: be bitter or forgive. It is not about getting our right to justice; that is God's job. It is about forgiving others as the Lord has forgiven us.

Lord, when I am treated unfairly give me grace to forgive.

Our Assigned Cross

★ ★ ★ ★ ★

READ LUKE 9:23-27.

Jesus told His followers to take up their cross daily and follow Him. Then He explained, "For whoever would save his life will lose it, but whoever loses his life for my sake will save it" (Luke 9:23–24 ESV). For the Christian, taking up our cross means loss.

The Bible assures us that we have been saved by grace; it is not our actions or our circumstances that bring us salvation. But a personal encounter with the Crucified does mean carrying our assigned cross and walking our own path of suffering for Christ. For some, that may mean enduring criticism from friends or loved ones. For others, that may even include persecution or martyrdom.

When God allows us the high calling of carrying our cross, will we be as eager to follow the Crucified as when we follow Him as the Rescuer, Strong Tower, and Healer? For all who follow the Crucified, there is no other way home.

Whether my cross is light or heavy, grant me today the needed courage and strength to bear it.

He Can Do the Impossible

★ ★ ★ ★ ★

READ GENESIS 18:9–15.

Sometimes we think that we know what's best for our lives. We make plans and do our best to prepare ourselves for the outcome we want to attain. Yet when our plans go awry, we realize that we don't know what's best for us. Only God does. And sometimes His plans take us through the territory of the impossible.

The Old Testament patriarch Abraham most likely didn't imagine that he would be changing diapers at the ripe old age of one hundred. But God knew what was best for them. Sarah's response of laughter when she learned of God's decision to give them a child in their old age showed that she doubted God could do the impossible. But He could—and He did.

Do you trust God to not only know what's best for you but also to do the impossible? Are you willing to journey with Him even if He changes your plans and takes you to a place you once thought impossible?

Jesus, I trust You to do the impossible.

Serious about Heavenly Joy

★ ★ ★ ★ ★

READ PSALM 66.

What motivated Jesus to die for us? Was it love? The Bible says, "Greater love has no one than this, than to lay down one's life for his friends" (John 15:13 NKJV). Was it obedience to God? Scripture tells us, "[Jesus] humbled himself by becoming obedient to death—even death on a cross" (Philippians 2:8). Was it to satisfy God's wrath against sin and evil? "God set [Christ] forth as a propitiation by His blood" (Romans 3:25 NKJV).

These verses all help answer the question: why was Jesus crucified on our behalf? Yet the Bible also tells us another reason that Jesus stayed on the cross when He could have called many angels to His aid—joy. "Jesus...for the joy that was set before Him endured the cross, despising the shame" (Hebrews 12:2 NKJV).

If joy is the business of heaven, should it not also be the serious business of earth?

Keep me from glib living and guide me into the serious joy
of Your steadfast love!

Individual Preferences

★ ★ ★ ★ ★

READ HEBREWS 11:1-16.

Ask college students how they ended up attending their school, and you'll receive a variety of responses. Some students will say their parents graduated from there. Some will say they followed siblings or sweethearts. Others will talk about scholarships or desired fields of study.

Similarly, Christians have a variety of preferences for forms of worship and ministry. Some people like the worship style of their parents' congregation, while others prefer more modern music. Some serve God in simple, everyday acts of service, while others serve God in more visible, exciting ways. Trying to force our modes of worship and preferences of ministry on others will only backfire. Traditional hymns may be used to worship God or Christian rock may be. Private devotional time may be one person's favorite time of the day, whereas another may look forward to leading a group Bible study.

As long as God is the focus for worship, that's what counts.

Lord, help me to never place Your creativity in a box.

The Blessed Life

★ ★ ★ ★

READ PSALM 37:4.

The movie *Chariots of Fire* tells the story of Eric Liddell, a Scottish Christian born to missionary parents in China who competes for God's glory on the track in the 1924 Olympics.

After Eric misses a prayer meeting, his sister—who disapproves of his athletic pursuits—questions just how much his running really honors God. "I believe that God made me for a purpose," Eric responds. "But He also made me fast, and when I run, I feel His pleasure."

The activities we enjoy are blessings from God. Liddell eventually returned to China, and upon his death, all of Scotland mourned. His was indeed a blessed life.

Find those pursuits where you feel God's pleasure—and you, too, will be blessed.

Lord, help me to feel Your pleasure.

The Destination

★ ★ ★ ★ ★

READ JEREMIAH 29:11.

Using a road map or following the directions on a GPS helps us go from point A to point B with relative ease. But when we set off on our own trying to locate a destination using only our sense of direction, we often end up going in circles, backtracking, and generally getting stressed out.

Submission to God is a lot like using a road map. He knows the path we should travel and He's ready to be our guide. We shouldn't try to make the journey on our own—we are not wise enough to get ourselves out of the pitfalls and dead ends that show up as we travel. We need His help!

As we submit to God in all circumstances, we not only reach our destination but we experience contentment and joy in the journey. And through submission, we will one day reach our ultimate destination—kneeling before the throne of God, where true contentment will be ours forever.

I want to follow You, Lord, in perfect submission to Your will.

....

....

....

....

....

....

....

....

....

A Treasured Possession

★ ★ ★ ★

READ DEUTERONOMY 7:6–9.

The Bible describes the Israelites as a stiff-necked people. Often prideful and stubborn, they chose to go their own way time after time. They were a small nation, yet God made them mighty. They were foolish, yet God trusted them with His Word. They were unfaithful, yet God continually drew them back, rescuing them when they called out to Him for help.

A human father might tire of the antics of such a rebellious child, but the Lord refused to break His covenant with His children. The Israelites couldn't earn His love after their failures, because they had not earned it in the beginning. They were a holy people only because God made them holy. He treasured them, and it was because of His grace that He remained faithful toward them despite their wayward spirits. He chose them and bought them, and because of His great love He refused to abandon them. He feels the same way about us today.

Help me stop striving, Lord, and rest secure in Your love.

A Paradigm Shift

★ ★ ★ ★ ★

READ HEBREWS 13:20-21.

What do you hurry to do each day? Sometimes we rush through the activities of our day to get to what we think is the best part: quitting time, mealtime, bedtime. We don't have to be forced to do the tasks we really want to do: play a sport we love, spend time with our family, read a good book. We give to the tasks we love our best energy and purpose.

Does the performance of "every good work" stir the same energy and readiness of mind? If we're honest, we'll probably say, "Not always." Sometimes we approach our service to the Lord with reluctance, knowing the limitations of our strength or desire. But it's time to make a paradigm shift. We can readily "perform every good work" when we know that the God of peace equips us. Relying on His limitless strength instead of our flagging energy or desire enables us to rejoice in the tasks to which He has called us.

Ready to rejoice? Rely on God.

Stir me, Lord, to the good works You would have me do.

A Heart for God

★ ★ ★ ★ ★

READ 1 JOHN 1:8–2:3.

Failure can be very painful. Even the most highly trained athletes cannot hide the agony of failure on their faces. The higher the hopes—Super Bowl, World Series, or Stanley Cup—the greater the portrait of loss. When the camera pans the losing team with their blank stares, we see their hearts: "We've lost. It's over. We've failed." Then we observe the winning team with bright smiles on their faces, and we grasp their hearts: "We've won. It's ours. We've succeeded!"

As much as in winning, in losing we can see the true heart of a champion. This is especially true when it comes to our moral failure—when we stumble and sin, we discover our true character. Instead of wallowing in the pain of self-condemnation, the next step for a Christian is to turn back to God in repentance. The heart of a moral champion is a heart that longs for God's.

When I sin, I will trust Your forgiveness, Jesus,
to fully restore my heart.

Unlikely Kings

★ ★ ★ ★ ★

READ REVELATION 4:4–11.

The Bible provides two unlikely snapshots of royalty. One focuses on a thief dying on a wooden cross. While the crowd jeered, the thief dared to believe that the man next to him—Jesus—had a kingdom waiting for Him and could take him to an eternal paradise (Luke 23:39–43). The second comes in the fourth chapter of Revelation where believers in heaven cast their crowns before the throne of God. Because of Jesus, the unlikely are made kings in a place they would have no hope of gaining without Him.

Through God's grace, you too will someday bear a crown that no one can take away. Salvation, the guarantee of your future inheritance, clothes you with royal authority like a kingly mantle. God chose you to rule with Him.

On a day when you might feel helpless or powerless, remember that you're royalty—you're a child of the King!

Lord, I am excited for the future when I will reign with You.

....

....

....

....

....

....

....

....

....

....

Bear One Another's Burdens

★ ★ ★ ★ ★

READ 2 CORINTHIANS 1:3–5.

Dick and Rick Hoyt love marathons. They run as a team, father and son. The 2009 Boston Marathon was their one thousandth race. That isn't the only remarkable thing about them, though.

Dick Hoyt is almost seventy years old, and Rick Hoyt has had cerebral palsy since birth. Dick pushes his son's wheelchair every inch of every race. Rick depends on his father, but Dick gets a whole lot of encouragement from his son.

We need one another. People around us are hurting, and sometimes the pain can become overwhelming. At those times, we need to put our hurts on the back burner so that we can help others. Then, when the time comes, they will give us a place to lean as well.

And in front of us is the glory of the finish line.

God, help me to support those who need my help today.

Prayers of an Aching Heart

★ ★ ★ ★ ★

READ ROMANS 8:26–27.

We may find it difficult to pray. It's not that we don't want to pray; in times of distress, we know we need God more than ever! But when our heart is breaking, prayer sometimes seems impossible. We may turn toward God, but in our anguish we can't even form the words to express our sorrow.

God provided the Holy Spirit to be our comforter. In those times when our hearts are aching and our vision is clouded by confusion and grief, the Spirit comes close to us and wraps us in the soothing embrace of God's presence. When we are overwhelmed beyond words, the Spirit takes our unformed prayers to God on our behalf.

When your heart is breaking, remember that God is near to comfort you.

Thank You for being near and hearing the cries of my heart, Lord.

By His Hands

★ ★ ★ ★ ★

READ JOHN 1:1–5.

When you view the magnificence of the Grand Canyon or the wonder of Victoria Falls, perhaps you can easily picture a big God who created such breathtaking beauty. Gaze upon your own hands, whether thin fingered or work roughened. Could your hands create such wonders?

Jesus's hands could. Though Jesus was a carpenter with calloused hands, the apostle John proclaimed Him to be the one by whom all things were made. Jesus Christ was both man and God. By His word the beluga whale and the butterfly sprang into being. And during His incarnation, the power of creation was evident in His hands as He miraculously turned water into wine, calmed the raging sea, and turned one boy's meager lunch into a feast for well over five thousand people.

The next time you look at your hands, consider what Jesus, the eternal creator and sustainer of all things, can do with them.

Use my hands, Lord, to do what needs to be done.

Giving Him Our All

★ ★ ★ ★ ★

READ MATTHEW 25:14-29.

Perhaps one of the most difficult lessons of the Christian faith is that this life is temporary yet what we do in it has eternal consequences. Jesus said, "For whoever desires to save his life will lose it, but whoever loses his life for My sake will find it" (Matthew 16:25 NKJV). Scripture is full of examples of this truth. The same principle holds true when it comes to how we treat others and what we give them spiritually.

We have been blessed with an eternal reward far outweighing what we deserve—our salvation in Christ. By giving away the love and care that Christ has given us, we know that our efforts will not only have consequences on this planet but will also have eternal results. Giving Him our lives and our passions ensures that they will be used for greater gain.

Let's be eager to share what we have been given, knowing that Christ has greater plans for it than we could ever imagine.

Help me to give freely of the love You have given me, Jesus.

The Finish Line

★ ★ ★ ★ ★

READ JAMES 1:2-8.

On October 20, 1968, the Mexico City Olympic Stadium was both the starting line and the finish line of the Olympic marathon. During the race, John Stephen Akhwari of Tanzania stumbled and seriously hurt his leg. Medics bandaged the man's bloody calf, and then Akhwari rose and began to hobble forward. Though in agonizing pain, Akhwari continued, mile after mile. As he finally entered the stadium, he completed the final lap, hobbling all the way. The crowd rose and cheered, but Akhwari simply finished the lap and left the stadium. Later, a sportswriter asked, "Why didn't you just quit?" Akhwari responded, "My country did not send me seven thousand miles to start the race. It sent me to finish the race."

Our God finishes what He starts. James tells us perseverance must "finish its work" (James 1:4 NKJV, italics added) so that we can be mature in our righteousness. Let us also complete the good work we start.

Lord, give me the strength to be like You—
someone who completes good work.

Cause and Effect

★ ★ ★ ★ ★

READ PSALM 29:1-2.

Cause and effect is simple. Every junior-high science student understands that adding some substances to others creates a reaction—sometimes positive, sometimes negative. You might get a compound of beautiful color and scent; you might get an explosion.

How we worship is based on why we worship—cause and effect. Are we worshiping because it's the thing to do, our friends do it, it's a habit? If so, our worship will be stale, flat, emotionless. In fact, it might not be true worship at all.

However, if we are worshiping because of our love for this God who saves us, transforms us, and promises us eternity, then our worship will reach to heaven and bring us close to Him. To worship God as He should be worshiped, we need to focus completely on who He is and what He has done. Cause and effect.

Here I am, Lord. Empty me of myself and fill me with You.

Shine On

★ ★ ★ ★ ★

READ EXODUS 10:21-23.

Moses stretched out his hand and darkness covered Egypt. Not a rosy dusk. Not a sapphire twilight. Darkness so deep you couldn't see an inch into the blackness. Agonizing, claustrophobic, crushing darkness.

"Yet all the Israelites had light in the places where they lived" (Exodus 10:23 NIV). In the midst of the plague of darkness, the light of the presence of the Lord shone on His chosen ones. God's light pierced the darkness, appearing even brighter against the oppression surrounding it. Life-giving, liberating, sustaining light.

Many people are lost in darkness so deep that they can't see a way out. But when we shine the light and love of Christ, they can't help but notice. Our testimony is a valuable thing, but sometimes, more than our words, people need to see the presence of the Lord reflected in our lives, directing them to the Light of the world.

May my light shine today, Lord, drawing others to You.

Eager to Fill

★ ★ ★ ★ ★

READ PSALM 16:9-11.

Jesus wept and laughed. He fed the multitudes and taught thousands. He grew angry at the moneychangers and welcomed the children with open arms. He expressed many emotions during His ministry on earth, but He was the most gentle and tender toward those who came to Him simply to worship Him, soaking in His presence.

Mary of Bethany, who sat and listened at His feet, earned a place of honor. Jesus defended the woman who came to Him and drenched His feet with her tears, saying she wanted only to be near Him and worship Him.

Each of these believers came to Jesus to worship Him—to pour out their longings, their fears, and their devotion to Him. In return, Jesus eagerly filled them with His love, His healing, and His peace.

Spending time worshiping Jesus unites His heart with yours. When you draw near to Him, He responds by eagerly filling you with His presence and love.

Unite my heart with Yours, Lord. Fill me with Your presence and love.

Finding Home

★ ★ ★ ★ ★

READ HEBREWS 12:7–11.

The prodigal son envisioned a life of entertainment and pleasure outside the confines of his country home. He longed to broaden his horizons beyond his boring life and the watchful eye of his father. So he demanded his inheritance and struck out on his own. But he squandered his wealth, lived a wild existence, and returned home broken and humbled.

Before, the boundaries of his father's land had felt confining. Now the son longed for the security of home. Once, his father's wealth had given him all the food he needed. But the inheritance only fed his folly. Previously, his father's arms made him struggle for liberty; now they offered protection.

The son learned the difficult lesson that freedom comes within the margins of lovingly set boundaries.

Our loving Father also gives us limits. His boundaries are not to keep us in but to keep danger and evil out. His rules are not to limit us but to sustain us. Within His walls we find acceptance and provision. In His arms, we find our home.

Father, help me to feel and know and submit to Your loving boundaries.

Unmasking the Impossible

★ ★ ★ ★ ★

READ JEREMIAH 32:17–19.

It's impossible," we say with a resigned sigh. We can't see a way out. All the choices lead to unpleasant results—if there are any choices at all. We may be tempted to give up in despair. What a change of perspective, then, when we see that impossible situation as an opportunity from God that has merely been brilliantly disguised!

God wants us to look at our difficult situations as if we were attending a masquerade party—what we think is impossible and scary is merely an illusion. Like the moment of unmasking at a party, it's time to reveal the true identity of what has appeared to be an impossible situation—opportunity.

Take off opportunity's disguise today. As you unmask your impossible situation and reveal it as an opportunity from God, the greatness of God is just waiting to show itself in your life.

Open my eyes to see Your opportunity in my difficult situation, God.

Promptings to Prayer

★ ★ ★ ★ ★

READ LUKE 22:39–46.

A refrain heard regularly from new Christians who are learning the practice of prayer is, "I don't know what to pray about." This is something we all struggle with periodically as we seek to draw closer to God in prayer throughout our Christian journeys.

Yet God allows many circumstances in our world and in our individual lives to serve as promptings to prayer. He speaks to us through our friends, relatives, and even those we might view as our enemies. He speaks to us through a pastor's sermon, radio message, or book. He even speaks to us through our illnesses and our difficulties. He also speaks to us through things for which we should pray.

Ultimately, through our prayer, God wants us to spend more time with Him, to draw closer to Him, and to see and sense His heart. He uses things all around us to prompt us to pray, and He earnestly desires that our prayers lead us closer to Him.

Give me a sense of Your heart, Father,
so that my prayer life draws me closer to You.

Unlocked Potential

★ ★ ★ ★ ★

READ 1 CORINTHIANS 12:27–31.

Go into any local bookstore and you'll find shelves lined with self-help books that tout the authors' ability to unlock the potential of a person. And in sold-out conference centers and arenas, motivational speakers assure us that if we would just follow these seven steps or buy this product, we will notice a difference in our lives in a matter of days. Or so we are told.

Yet God alone is the ultimate locksmith of our hearts. He can unlock potential no one even dreamed of, because He put it there. He has given each of us specific gifts and abilities and dreams. He knows the full measure of our potential. Best of all, He doesn't assign an "expiration date" or an age limit for the realization of that potential. You can be all that God calls you to be whenever God wills.

Lay your heart before the One who knows it better than even you do. Let Him unlock your potential.

Lord, guide me in the way You would have me go.

The Event Coordinator

★ ★ ★ ★ ★

READ MATTHEW 6:9–13.

When we have a jam-packed schedule, it's easy to fall into the trap of approaching the day like a busy event coordinator. Excited about our plans, our prayer—if we make time to offer one—becomes a passionate monologue telling God everything we're going to do that day. We approach God looking for His stamp of approval on our plans instead of asking for His direction.

But oh, the blessing that comes when we let God be the Event Coordinator and humbly take our place as His assistant. When we give control of our daily schedule to God, things may not turn out exactly as we would have planned, but isn't God the ultimate planner? He is omniscient, omnipotent, and omnipresent—attributes that make Him the greatest Event Coordinator possible. No matter how capable we are, God is infinitely more capable.

Ask Him to not only fulfill His plan for you but lead that plan. Do more than just include Him in your plans—let Him be in charge.

Fulfill Your plans for me today, Lord.

True Light

★ ★ ★ ★ ★

READ JOHN 1:9-18.

Ever worry about how to share your faith? Perhaps you worry not only about who you'll talk to but what you'll say and how you'll say it. The good news is that God does the bulk of the work in spreading the good news. As you share your faith with others, He not only reminds you of the truth but He also shines His light through you.

The apostle John wrote of Jesus as the Light who revealed Himself to a people trapped in darkness. While some preferred the darkness, others gravitated toward the light of His truth. The more they sought the light, the more they saw how splendid it was and how desperately they needed it. After His resurrection, Jesus sent the Holy Spirit to help bear witness of His truth to them and to you.

Ask God to show you someone you can talk with about your faith. The Holy Spirit will help you be a light in a dark world.

Here I am, Lord. Please send me to share Your light with others.

Come with Me

★ ★ ★ ★ ★

READ MARK 6:30–32.

Jesus was a busy man. Healing the sick, casting out demons, teaching, traveling, and communing with His Father kept Him busy from dawn until the evening hours. But Jesus frequently pulled away from the crowds. He was fully God yet fully man—and as a human being, He needed time to physically rest and recharge.

Sometimes He invited His friends to come along with Him into the quiet places. He used these times of solitude with His disciples to explain, to mentor, and to train. Away from the crowds, Jesus taught them the meanings of His parables and shared secrets. His followers used these times to ask questions, to seek answers, and to share their deepest thoughts with their Teacher.

Jesus still longs for quiet time with us so He can teach and train us. It is in these times of quiet rest that He addresses the deepest stirrings of our hearts.

Bless my time of quiet with You today, Lord.
I want to hear from You.

The Value of Being Available

★ ★ ★ ★ ★

READ 1 CORINTHIANS 1:26–31.

The Bible shows us over and over that God favors the unfavorable. He guided a nation to freedom through a stuttering shepherd. He placed the king's crown on the head of a gangly teenager. He delivered His people through an orphan girl turned unlikely queen.

Jesus desired the undesirable. He broke bread with tax collectors and prostitutes. He touched the unclean and infirm. He conversed with foreigners and children. He used ordinary people to spread the good news of His message.

Jesus doesn't require His followers to be able, just to be available. When Jesus enters the lives of those who are foolish, weak, lowly, or despised and changes them, people notice. All throughout history God has used weak and broken vessels to accomplish great things for His glory. And He still does.

I know that if I make myself available to Your plans, God,
You will make me able. Thank You.

One Day at a Time

★ ★ ★ ★ ★

READ MATTHEW 11:25-30.

How can we possibly stay on track spiritually in all of life's ups and downs? How can we know that we'll be able to stay faithful to God tomorrow when we have no idea what tomorrow will bring—much less next month or next year?

A Chinese proverb says that the journey of a thousand miles begins with a single step. So it is with life. We do not know what the future holds, but we trust God and walk into it one step at a time. If we are faithful in this moment, and then faithful in the next moment, and so on and so on, we will build up to a life of spiritual faithfulness.

And what does that faithfulness look like? It is simply coming to Jesus, staying close to Him, seeking to honor Him in all we do—in the strength He Himself gives. All of these obedient steps will add up to a life of faithfulness.

Today I come to You, Jesus. Teach me in every moment.

Mine!

READ ROMANS 10:14–17.

One of the first words a young child learns to say is "Mine!" We never outgrow our desire to claim what's ours. We jealously guard our family time or our leisure time. We keep a tight grip on our possessions.

This tendency to mark what's ours sometimes extends to faith. We talk about owning our faith. But faith is a gift from God just as life itself is. As the apostle Paul explains, our faith comes through hearing the Word of the Lord.

Romans 10:17 and Ephesians 2:8 remind us that salvation is a gift offered to us from God. Through the acceptance of this gift, God looks at you in love and says, "Mine."

When you belong to God, everything you have is His: your possessions, your time, yourself. Why not offer all to God today?

Lord, thank You for Your love that claims me.
All that I have and all that I am is Yours.

The Holy Spirit's Care for Us

★ ★ ★ ★ ★

READ ROMANS 8:11–17.

All of us experience periods of difficulty and pain in our lives—times when we wonder what God has in store for us. These times can also feel particularly lonely, as we seem to struggle to determine the path God has prepared for us.

Yet in these painful times, as well as during periods of comfort and satisfaction, we must never forget that the Holy Spirit continues to indwell our hearts. He lives in us as One who cares deeply about everything in our lives.

His indwelling serves an eternal purpose, as well. For at all times in our lives, the infinite Holy Spirit is guiding us, caring for us, and ultimately deepening our connection to Him as our physical bodies become His holy temples.

Let's not underestimate the refining and care the Holy Spirit is undertaking in our daily lives. His ceaseless love is unmatched, and He will never leave His people.

Please refine my life to make me more like You, Lord.

God's Embrace

★ ★ ★ ★ ★

READ PSALM 46:1-11.

Concerts. Churches. Festivals. Football stadiums. What do they have in common? Huge crowds. Ironically, though, at any of these events, it's possible—easy, even—to feel alone. It's no secret that humans can feel lonely anywhere. Most of us will go to any length to make a connection. Some of us seek it through romance, others through popularity, and still others through social networks or online games. Connecting is one of our most desperate longings, and we'll strive for it wherever we can get it.

But there's a problem: no matter where we try to find it, true connection will elude us if we seek it in anything but God. For a time, these intimacy substitutes will satisfy, but inevitably they will leave us unfulfilled.

With God, however, we are never alone. As our Comforter, He is close to us, arms stretched out, ready to hold us. Embrace Him. He won't let go.

Father, hold me. I do not want to be alone.

Only in Weakness

★ ★ ★ ★ ★

READ JUDGES 7.

Gideon farmed. Moses led sheep. Martha bustled and served. The disciples fished. Then God came calling.

God used Gideon to grow an army. He told Moses to lead His people. Jesus told Martha to sit and learn. The disciples left their nets and fished for men.

God removed each of them—and many others—from their comfortable, ordinary existence and propelled them into ministry opportunities that stretched them beyond their natural talents. They learned new skills. They went new places. At times while they served God out of their weakness, they stumbled and He caught them. God put them into circumstances that forced them to depend on Him.

Security and aptitude often breed autonomy. But God knows that dependence and uncertainty foster reliance, and reliance fosters relationship. So He often calls us out of our comfort zones to learn that it is only through His strength that we are made strong and only through His provision that we accomplish great deeds.

I surrender my talents, God, knowing You will equip me for every good work.

Ellie Claire® Gift & Paper Expressions
Franklin, TN 37067
EllieClaire.com

Ellie Claire is a registered trademark of Worthy Media, Inc.

Here I am, Lord
© 2017 by Ellie Claire
Published by Ellie Claire, an imprint of Worthy Publishing Group, a division
of Worthy Media, Inc.

ISBN 978-1-63326-168-6

The Holy Bible, New King James Version® (NKJV). Copyright © 1982 by
Thomas Nelson, Inc. The Holy Bible, English Standard Version® (ESV®),
copyright © 2001 by Crossway Bibles, a publishing ministry of Good News
Publishers. The New American Standard Bible® (NASB), Copyright © 1960,
1962, 1963, 1968, 1971, 1972, 1973, 1975, 1977, 1995 by The Lockman
Foundation.

Stock or custom editions of Ellie Claire titles may be purchased in bulk for
educational, business, ministry, fund-raising, or sales promotional use. For
information, please e-mail info@EllieClaire.com

Cover and interior design by Bart Dawson

Cover illustrations: Shutterstock.com

Printed in China

1 2 3 4 5 6 7 8 9 –RRD– 21 20 19 18 17

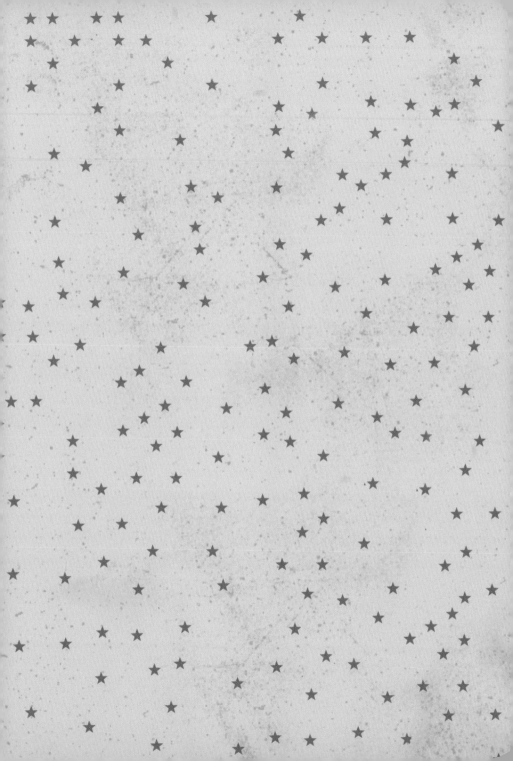

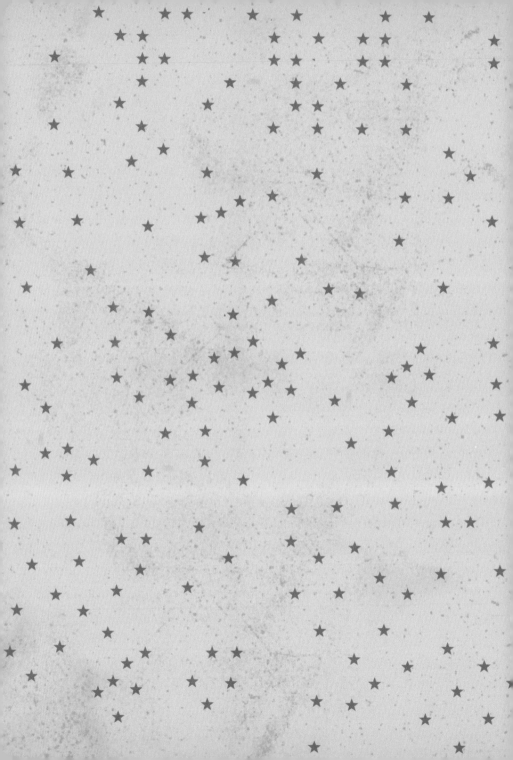